OSPREY AIRCRAFT OF THE ACES • 84

American Nightfighter Aces of World War 2

SERIES EDITOR: TONY HOLMES

OSPREY AIRCRAFT OF THE ACES • 84

American Nightfighter Aces of World War 2

Andrew Thomas and Warren Thompson

OSPREY
PUBLISHING

Front Cover
Between May and July 1945, the Japanese threw everything they had into the air in a last ditch attempt to cripple the massive Allied fleet of ships that was concentrated around the island of Okinawa. Aircraft attacked these vessels both day and night, and a handful of nightfighter units were charged with repulsing the raids after dark. Future ace Maj R Bruce Porter became CO of Marine Corps nightfighter squadron VMF(N)-542 on Okinawa on 22 May, the pilot joining the unit with three kills to his name following a tour with VMF-121 on Guadalcanal in 1943. Looking for two victories to make him an ace, Porter finally got his chance on the night of 15 June.

Flying his personal F6F-5N Hellcat BuNo 78669 *Black Death*, he set off on a patrol from the airfield on Ie Shima. 'The night was completely dark – there was no moonlight whatsoever, and an extremely thick cloud cover', Porter recalled in his autobiography, *Ace! A Marine Nightfighter Pilot in World War 2*. Climbing to an altitude of 10,000 ft, he was 45 minutes into the mission when he was vectored onto a twin-engined Japanese Ki-45 'Nick' by his Ground Control Intercept officer, call-sign 'Handyman'. Switching on his fighter's wingtip-mounted AN/APS-6 centrimetric radar, Porter followed the tiny orange blip that appeared on the display screen in his cockpit until he caught sight of the fighter's exhaust flames. He promptly shot the aircraft down from close range.

Returning to his patrol line, Porter maintained his position off the northern coast of Okinawa for another hour before 'Handyman' announced that he had a second contact. As he closed on the target, seeking visual identification, he could tell by the flames coming from its exhaust stacks that it was a G4M 'Betty' bomber, but there was something very different about it. When just 250 ft away from the contact, Porter realised that the 'Betty' had a Baka flying-bomb attached to its belly. The intruder was trying to get close enough to the fleet to release its manned suicide weapon.

'I drifted upward a bit to get a good belly shot. By the time I reached a comfortable height, I had closed to within 250 ft. Then I slowly squeezed both triggers (Porter's F6F-5N Hellcat was the only one in the squadron fitted with a pair of 20 mm cannon and four 0.50-cal machine guns). After only a second or two the wing fuel tanks ignited in a garish explosion, and the sky in front of my windscreen was filled with an expanding ball of flame. What a night! "Handyman" and I had scored a rare double night kill, and I had fulfilled my fondest ambition as a fighter pilot. I was an Ace!' (*Cover artwork by Mark Postlethwaite*)

First published in Great Britain in 2008 by Osprey Publishing
Midland House, West Way, Botley, Oxford, OX2 0PH
443 Park Avenue South, New York, NY, 10016, USA
E-mail; info@ospreypublishing.com

ISBN 13: 978 1 84603 306 3

Edited by Tony Holmes & Bruce Hales-Dutton
Page design by Tony Truscott
Cover Artwork by Mark Postlethwaite
Aircraft Profiles by Chris Davey
Index by Alison Worthington
Originated by PDQ Media Digital Media Solutions
Printed in Hong Kong through Bookbuilders

08 09 10 11 12   10 9 8 7 6 5 4 3 2 1

For a catalogue of all books published by Osprey please contact:
NORTH AMERICA
Osprey Direct, C/o Random House Distribution Center,
400 Hahn Road, Westminster, MD 21157
E-mail:info@ospreydirect.com

ALL OTHER REGIONS
Osprey Direct UK, PO Box 140 Wellingborough, Northants, NN8 2FA, UK
E-mail: info@ospreydirect.co.uk
www.ospreypublishing.com

ACKNOWLEDGEMENTS
The authors wish to thank Robert Bolinder, Tom Cunningham, Jane Dear, Pat Dellamano, Bill Hess, James F Luma DFC, David Powers, Russ Reiserer, Gp Capt R D Schultz DFC CD, Barrett Tillman, Flt Lt V A Williams DFC and the staff at the Tailhook Association for their help with this book.

CONTENTS

CHAPTER ONE
GROPING IN THE DARK 6

CHAPTER TWO
SERVING THE KING 13

CHAPTER THREE
YANKS IN BEAUS 31

CHAPTER FOUR
ENTER THE BLACK WIDOW 55

CHAPTER FIVE
'A DANGEROUS BUSINESS' 73

APPENDICES 89
COLOUR PLATES COMMENTARY 91
BIBLIOGRAPHY 95
INDEX 96

GROPING IN THE DARK

As Europe rearmed during the late 1930s, aircraft manufacturers of the likely protagonists were designing ever more capable fighters and bombers, while purchasing commissions from Britain and France were also looking for combat types from other sources, particularly the USA.

At the same time, scientists in Britain and Germany were developing new weapons and equipment such as radio direction finding (RDF, or radar as it was later named) usually under a cloak of great secrecy. Emerging threats provided the impetus for new ideas about the use of air power, as well as for aircraft design. This led to huge increases in performance, especially of day fighters, resulting in world-class designs like the Supermarine Spitfire and Messerschmitt Bf 109.

But both Britain and Germany also considered the night defence of their homelands, although it was presumed that this could be left to single-seat or long-range twin-engined day fighters adapted for a nocturnal role. By the end of the decade, therefore, RAF Fighter Command could deploy several squadrons of Blenheim light bombers converted for the nightfighter role through the addition of an under-fuselage pack of four Browning 0.303-in machine guns. Designated the Mk IF, these aircraft were subsequently officially classified as dual-role day and nightfighters.

With its long east coast exposed to Germany just across the North Sea, Britain was particularly concerned about the possibility of night raids in

The first RAF nightfighter to be equipped with radar was the converted Blenheim IF. The aerials for the early radar (AI Mk III in this particular aircraft) were carried on the nose and above and below the port outer wing. These machines gained a few successes, and were later used for nightfighter training – this Blenheim IF (K7159) was assigned to No 54 OTU at Church Fenton in 1941 (*P H T Green collection*)

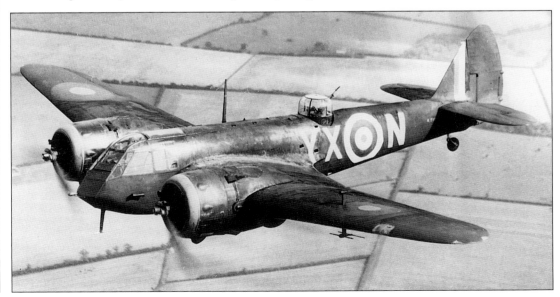

the event of war. The development of the long-range Chain Home radar system around the coastline was well advanced, but the problem of directing a fighter to a target hidden by darkness or bad weather continued to exercise scientists' minds. A radar set small enough to be carried aloft was eventually developed, but the need for a specialist on-board operator meant a multi-seat aircraft. So, in November 1938, Blenheim I L6622 of the Aeroplane & Armament Experimental Establishment (A&AEE) was allocated to airborne radar development work. It was later to be joined by several more.

On 17 July 1939 the first-ever order for AI (Air Intercept) Radar Mk III was made by the Air Ministry, with the intention being to equip 21 Blenheim IFs. By the end of the month the first aircraft, readily identified by nose 'arrowhead' and wing dipole aerials, had been delivered to No 25 Sqn, based at Northolt on the western edges of Greater London. By the outbreak of war, the RAF could deploy 15 AI-equipped Blenheim IFs. Shortly afterwards, several were issued to Nos 600 and 604 Sqns, with the former detaching three aircraft to Manston, on the Kent coast, in an attempt to intercept enemy seaplanes laying mines in the shipping lanes of the Thames Estuary. But it soon became apparent that when flying at low level, radar returns from the ground – known as 'clutter' – masked the low-flying intruders. Little was achieved.

By mid-April 1940 the Fighter Interception Unit (FIU) had been formed at Tangmere with radar-equipped Blenheim IFs to continue development of equipment and tactics. The unit took delivery of the improved AI Mk IV radar for its aircraft, and on the night of 22/23 July, as the Battle of Britain raged, Flg Off Glyn Ashfield achieved the first successful radar-guided night interception. At the controls of L6836, he destroyed a Dornier Do 17 of 2./KG 3 off the Sussex coast near Brighton.

Despite this victory, the RAF quickly realised that the Blenheim IF lacked the performance and armament to be really effective. As autumn approached, and the Luftwaffe began its intensive night *Blitz* on Britain, the first examples of the pugnacious Bristol Beaufighter were delivered to

The RAF's first really effective nightfighter was the pugnacious Bristol Beaufighter. This Merlin-engined Mk IIF of No 409 Sqn clearly shows the early nose arrowhead and wing-mounted dipole antennae (*W Woodward*)

the RAF. These aircraft were immediately equipped with AI radar and deployed on night defence duties. As equipment and tactics improved, they gradually wrested the initiative from the enemy.

Meanwhile, across the Atlantic in the isolationist United States, such developments in the squabbling nations of Europe were viewed with interest but, in the absence of any direct threat to the Continental USA, little else. As a result, fighter design lagged behind that in Europe, and night defence was not even considered. And yet although there were no nightfighter pilots in the US Army Air Corps (which subsequently became the US Army Air Force in June 1941), a few Americans were able to gain nocturnal combat experience. Indeed, some US citizens joined the RAF or the Royal Canadian Air Force (RCAF) in late 1939, and the following year the RAF established its 'Eagle' squadrons, manned by American volunteers. These units, however, were exclusively equipped for day fighting, and it is not thought that any US citizens flew night-fighter sorties during the *Blitz*.

In 1941 the RCAF formed several nightfighter squadrons in Britain as part of its expansion. Among them was No 410 Sqn. Based at Ayr, in Scotland, it was equipped with Boulton Paul Defiant turret fighters and commanded by Sqn Ldr Paul Y Davoud, who had been born in Provost, Utah, and then moved to Canada with his widowed mother in 1926. In 1935 the 24-year-old Davoud arrived in England to train as a pilot with the RAF. He later returned to Canada, where he flew commercially before joining the RCAF in 1940. Davoud was taught the art of nocturnal warfare at No 60 Operational Training Unit (a specialist nightfighter training squadron formed in late April 1941 and equipped with Blenheims and Defiants), and he duly became the first American to command a nightfighter squadron during the war.

Meantime, as they realised the RAF was fighting a nocturnal battle with the Luftwaffe, US military leaders began laying the foundations of their own nightfighter units. The initial contract with Northrop to build the

When first formed, No 410 Sqn was equipped with the Boulton Paul Defiant I in which all the armament was concentrated in the power-operated turret. The unit's first CO was American-born Sqn Ldr P Y Davoud (*C E Brayshaw*)

P-61 Black Widow was signed in late January 1941, 11 months before the Japanese attack on Pearl Harbor. The resulting aircraft would not become operational until May 1944, however. This meant that at the time of its entry into the war, the USAAF lacked a specialised nightfighter, even though the RAF and the Luftwaffe were rapidly advancing the art of nocturnal aerial warfare.

Losses incurred during the daylight battles over England in the summer and autumn of 1940 had prompted the Luftwaffe to launch night attacks on London and other major English cities. This resulted in the so-called *Blitz* of 1940/41, which forced the RAF to respond with radar-equipped nightfighters.

Two years later, US forces found themselves in a similar position during 1942, when the Japanese were trying to dislodge the Marine Corps from its precarious toe-hold on the fetid island of Guadalcanal in the Solomons chain. Huge over-water distances, combined with the large number of enemy air bases, made the job of intercepting attacking Japanese aircraft at night a tough one. The tempo of such attacks increased as the US Navy and Marine Corps secured daytime air superiority over the island, and they continued for many months after the Marines had first waded ashore.

EARLY PACIFIC EXPERIENCE

Maj Carroll C Smith, CO of the 418th Nightfighter Squadron (NFS), was to become the leading US nightfighter ace in the Pacific theatre, scoring five kills flying the P-61 and two with the Lockheed P-38 Lightning. His comments place the early days of the American nightfighter programme into context;

'The war in the Pacific was totally different from that in Europe. There, we were up against the Axis powers, and they were smart, stubborn and dedicated to covering the areas they controlled, which included Western Europe and North Africa. But when you compare this area with the Pacific theatre it is indeed very small. In the Pacific, there were few land references over vast expanses of ocean, dotted with infrequent small islands. Some of these land masses were dangerous because of various mountainous regions, which could mean instant death in total darkness.

'We were very fortunate to have a handful of pilots who had experience from previous RAF service, and their nightfighting prowess was highly beneficial to the rest of us. Prior to 1940, there was a substantial amount of American military-based night flying but it wasn't on par with what would be needed in 1942. It involved a handful of military pilots trained by civilian airline pilots who used conventional radio aids and standard flight instruments. The glaring weakness in this was that few of these pilots were able to fly without visual reference to the ground. There were experiments in which flares and searchlights were used, but very little was gained that would have been of military value once we went up against the Japanese in the Solomons.'

At that stage of the war, the nightfighting techniques developed in Europe were some way ahead of those in the Pacific. Expertise, experience and tactics were slow to reach the latter theatre because the RAF's priority had been the defence of Britain. Although this was well understood by the Americans, they remained focused on finding a way of

Maj Carroll C Smith's 418th NFS operated the B-25H for a short period in 1944, before receiving examples of the brand new P-61 Black Widow. This photograph was taken at a base in New Guinea. Note the aircraft's overall flat black paint scheme (*George Kerstetter*)

preventing Japanese nocturnal incursions during the Guadalcanal and New Guinea campaigns. What they had already discovered was that night patrols over friendly airfields and ships was risky due to the separate chains of command for anti-aircraft artillery, ship-borne firepower and fighter units. These dangers had to be resolved before an effective nightfighter programme could reach maturity. Smith added;

'There were numerous entrenched "old Army" ideas which were hard to change. We were able to set up a combined system using our B-25s for

The P-70 Havoc proved to be a valuable training platform for future P-61 aircrews. A number of conventional A-20Gs like this particular aircraft were drafted in to help with the training of future nightfighter crews, as radar-equipped P-70s were always a little thin on the ground back in the USA. *SAD SACK* was assigned to the 348th NFS at the Orlando, Florida, training facility in 1942 (*Al Lukas*)

These war-weary 6th NFS P-70s were photographed on the PSP (Pierced-Steel Planking) parking area at Henderson Field, on Guadalcanal, in late 1943. Although by no means as suited to the nightfighting role as the RAF's Beaufighter or Mosquito or the Luftwaffe's Bf 110 or Ju 88, the Douglas 'twin' was the USAAF's principal nocturnal weapon of war until the P-61 was finally declared operational in May 1944 (*Al Lukas*)

night intruder missions in an effort to get the enemy aircraft before they took off from their own airfields. First, we had an outer ring away from friendly AAA that would consist of the P-70s and, later, the P-61s, which were under radar control. Then came a ring of Army anti-aircraft guns followed by P-38s at altitude working with the searchlights. This put several potential obstacles in the way of any enemy bombers trying to get through to a target.'

As the nightfighter programme in the Pacific built up momentum, the Allies were beginning to make small gains in their progress towards Japan. As USAAF, US Navy and Marine Corps units increased their daytime pressure on the Japanese, the enemy was forced to escalate its nocturnal efforts. Once US forward air strips units could be established following fierce fighting on Guadalcanal, Army and Marine Corps pilots could attack the Japanese, as well as continuing to defend friendly ground troops.

Similarly, the priority for US Navy fighter pilots was defence of the fleet, and especially the carriers from which increasingly damaging attacks on Japanese forces were being launched. With Allied air power growing each week, the emphasis for both sides shifted to night missions.

The US Navy's nightfighter programme was planned, established and led by a handful of gifted officers. One of them was Cdr R E 'Chick' Harmer, who would eventually act as godfather to the Navy's post-war nightfighter programme. Along the way he would command the first US carrier-based nightfighter unit, VF(N)-101, which was commissioned at Quonset Point, Rhode Island, in April 1943. Harmer offered an insight into the programme's early days;

'We received our first aircraft, which were F4U-1s, but they didn't have radar until a few months later. Until we could get up to speed with all of the necessary equipment, we were reduced to night drills and day gunnery missions in our "Dash-1s". At this early stage, we only had 14 pilots, and all but one were ensigns. We depended on F4F Wildcats to help these young pilots build up experience. They had to have at least ten hours of night-time and sixty hours of day-time experience.

'By the end of the year we had gained significant experience of working with radar, and our pilots had mastered the art of day-time carrier landings. But we hadn't yet gained any experience of night landings, and that was going to have to be our strongest point.

'It didn't seem long before we were ready for our first combat cruise aboard USS *Enterprise* (CV-6). Developing nightfighter tactics would be hard to do because you had to wait and see what the enemy was doing in order to counter them to best advantage. A stern approach was preferable under most conditions, but the phase of moon was an important factor.

'We found it was essential to keep the "bogey" between ourselves and the moon as the interception reached its final stages. It was fine for the approach to be made by radar and by visual contact from directly astern, but if the moon's phase and position were of possible assistance, we preferred an approach from the side so as to get the target directly up-moon from us. This would give our pilots the advantage in making visual contact before being spotted by the crew of the hostile aircraft.'

Once US and British nightfighters began operating effectively, the advance of the Axis powers was first slowed and then halted. From that point onwards, the Allies could begin their slow and costly journey to victory. Failure to develop successful aerial nightfighting equipment and tactics would have given the Axis an important advantage after dark at a crucial stage of the conflict, and this would have no doubt prolonged the war. The skills of this elite group of Allied aircrew ultimately proved to be instrumental in curtailing nocturnal operations by a determined enemy.

The P-61 Black Widow was the only Allied aircraft of World War 2 to be designed specifically for the nightfighter mission. The USAAF's largest frontline fighter was plagued by structural and radar problems in the early stages of its development, which prevented Northrop from delivering combat-capable P-61s to units in either the Pacific or Europe until the spring of 1944. This view of the pilot's position in the prototype XP-61 was taken at the Northrop plant in July 1943. Changes to the cockpit layout between the XP-61, YP-61 and production P-61As were minimal (*Gerald Balzer/Northrop*)

SERVING THE KING

The first four Defiant night-fighters were delivered from No 46 Maintenance Unit to the RCAF's Ayr-based No 410 Sqn on 8 July 1941. A week later, a further dozen examples of the single-engined four-gun turret-armed fighters had arrived. The squadron CO, Utah-born Sqn Ldr Paul Davoud, was then able to start bringing his unit up to an operational state. The first mission was flown on the 23rd when Davoud conducted a night-flying test in V1137/RA-K, which subsequently became his regular aircraft. He flew most days from then on, and on the 30th took part in a search for a missing Defiant, before going to stand-by.

No 410 Sqn's sister Defiant unit, No 409, based at Coleby Grange near Lincoln, became operational at the same time. Almost immediately, however, it began re-equipping with the Merlin-engined Beaufighter IIF. This variant of the powerful fighter could be quite tricky to handle, and on 2 September the unit's CO, Sqn Ldr N B Petersen, was killed during a conversion sortie. Paul Davoud arrived on the 6th to replace him, and he was to remain in command until February 1943. He set about supervising No 409 Sqn's conversion to the radar-equipped Beaufighter, which proved to be more effective than the Defiant, despite its handling problems.

The first American to command a nightfighter squadron, Wg Cdr Paul Davoud and his dog 'Beau' examine No 409 Sqn's 'scoreboard' fashioned from the propeller blade of one of the victims. Davoud claimed the unit's first success in November 1941 (*PAC*)

Splattered with mud, Beaufighter IIF T3145/KP-K of No 409 Sqn, seen here at Coleby Grange, was the regular aircraft of the CO, Wg Cdr P Y Davoud (*W Woodward*)

With the onset of long winter nights, Luftwaffe night raids began again in earnest, and success for No 409 Sqn, declared operational on 30 October, was not long in coming. On 1 November, Davoud, with his navigator Sgt T R Carpenter, shot down a Do 217 to claim the unit's first night victory and, it is thought, the war's first night kill by an American pilot. He described the combat, which took place over the North Sea off the Lincolnshire coast, in his combat report;

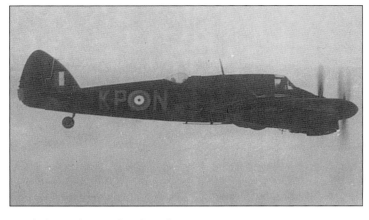

'I increased speed and turned to port and obtained a visual at 6000 ft (1850 m), silhouetted against the clouds in bright moonlight. I throttled back and lost height until slightly above and 400 yrd (370m) to the rear of the enemy aircraft, which dived for cloud cover. I closed to approximately 200 yrd (185 m), identified the bandit as a Do 217 and fired a short burst, observing hits on the starboard mainplane. The Dornier returned fire and, having closed to 200 yrd, I fired two long bursts, seeing the second burst hit its starboard engine. Just before the Dornier entered cloud, a big explosion blew its right engine and wing off. I pulled up to avoid a collision and the Dornier fell burning into the sea.'

Poor winter weather brought few further opportunities for action, and it was not until 10 December that Davoud (flying Beaufighter IIF R2320) gained another radar contact. He chased it for ten minutes, but the cloud cover was so thick that no visual contact was achieved.

No 409 Sqn's first Beaufighter VIFs arrived in early June 1942, and Davoud was in action again on 29 July when, with Plt Off Carpenter, he scrambled in X8162 to fly a patrol line off the coast at Skegness. Eight

In-flight views of operational Beaufighter IIs are rare, and this example from No 409 Sqn is believed to be R2320/KP-N, flown by Sgt D M Dixon. The Merlin-engined 'Beau' could prove a handful, and No 409 Sqn lost several in crashes (*D M Dixon*)

In June 1942 Wg Cdr Davoud's No 409 Sqn re-equipped with the Hercules-powered Beaufighter VIF, one of which was X8191/KP-P, pictured here. The nose and wing AI radar aerials can be clearly seen (*D M Dixon*)

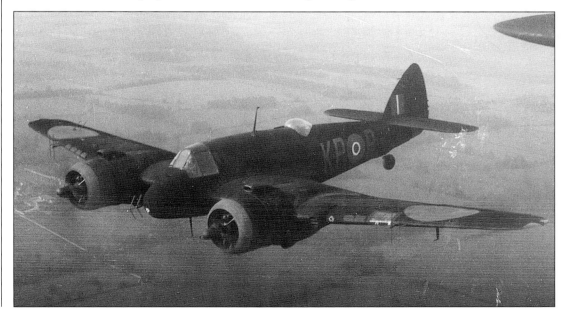

miles (13 km) east of the town they attacked an inbound He 111, which was claimed as probably destroyed. The pair continued their patrol, and a little later were vectored west. Over Grantham, they attacked and damaged a Do 217. It was Davoud's final claim, but he remained an inspirational commander, and was awarded the DFC for his leadership of No 409 Sqn before he left in early 1943.

NIGHT INTRUDERS

In early 1942, No 23 Sqn (which had previously flown Blenheim IFs) was based at Ford, on the Sussex coast, flying Douglas Havoc intruders against Luftwaffe bomber bases in France. On 17 February Flg Off Stanley J Cornforth was posted to the unit, the 26-year-old pilot from Pittsburgh, Pennsylvania, having joined the RAF in 1940. He began operations during April, at which point he was joined by another American serving in the RCAF. Sgt G R Wright flew his first operation in Havoc YP-U on 7 May when he bombed marshalling yards at Abbeville. Cornforth's first offensive operation came on the 30th of the month when, in YP-J, he headed for Gilze-Rijn, in Holland. There, he and his crew attacked dispersal areas. According to squadron records;

'Plt Off Cornforth and crew saw six enemy aircraft circling and flashing navigation lights before bombing the aerodrome. Another twin-engined aircraft was seen 20 miles (32 km) west of Gilze on the way home, but no combats resulted.'

It was the start of a busy period for the Pennsylvanian. He flew further intruder missions to Eindhoven and Pois, while Wright attacked trains near Montidier on the 9th. No 23 Sqn and its two American pilots saw plenty of action throughout the rest of June and into July. For the unit in general, great things were in the offing in the elegant shape of the Mosquito, to which it gradually converted. Cornforth's first Mosquito operation on the night of 22 August was uneventful, but five nights later Wright, flying Mosquito II YP-A, was busier, as his report described;

Photographed while on detachment at St Eval, Havoc I BT462/YP-Z of No 23 Sqn was first flown by one of the unit's successful American pilots, Sgt G R Wright, on an intruder mission to Beauvais on the night of 21 June 1942 (*Stuart Scott*)

Pictured immediately behind the seated figure of Mosquito ace Sqn Ldr 'Jackie' Starr is one of No 23 Sqn's successful American pilots, Flg Off Stanley Cornforth from Pittsburgh. He was lost while flying from Malta in April 1943 (*No 23 Squadron records*)

Flg Off Cornforth initially flew Havocs, before converting to the Mosquito II with No 23 Sqn. He flew DD712/YP-R on an intruder mission to Twente on 15 October 1942 (*via M J F Bowyer*)

'Whilst patrolling Bretigny, received intense and accurate Bofors fire. Whilst taking evasive action, aircraft were seen dispersed at Etaples/ Montdesit. An attack was made and one aircraft and a dispersal hut were destroyed.'

He was later credited with a Do 217 destroyed. The following night (28/29 August) Wright flew to Gilze-Rijn, where, as the unit's record book recorded, 'Sgt Wright (RCAF/US) attacked and damaged one unidentified aircraft as it was landing'. But this promising crew failed to return from their next sortie – an intruder mission over Holland on the night of 7/8 September. A few nights earlier, Cornforth had attacked a car near Etaples, but he saw little action until the end of the year, when the squadron moved to Malta.

By mid-1943 there was a large USAAF presence in Britain, and many young Americans who had originally joined the RAF or RCAF had transferred to the USAAF. The RAF's 'Eagle' squadrons were placed under US command in late 1942, although a few crews who were undergoing training for nightfighter duties were retained and seconded to British or Canadian squadrons. Among them was a 29-year-old from Jamesville, Ohio. Flt Off Archie Harrington had joined the RCAF in early 1941, but having been a bush pilot since he was 18, he was initially retained as an instructor. Then, on 22 June 1943, Harrington joined No 410 Sqn at Coleby Grange, where he arrived with a reputation for being a 'mad Yank' with a liking for low flying. His aggression and flying skill, however, would stand him in good stead.

Following a marked downturn in the tempo of German night attacks on Britain, some nightfighter units (including No 410 Sqn) were engaged in flying nocturnal offensive sorties known as 'Rangers', as well as 'Mahmoud' bomber support missions. Harrington flew his first operation – a bomber support sortie to Rennes – on 15 September.

The previous month, three more USAAF pilots had joined the squadron. They were Flt Offs O H Emmal from Hartford, Kansas, R N Geary from Santa Clara, California, and R L Wulfkuhlo. Emmal flew his first operational sortie on 23 September when he was scrambled from Coleby Grange, while Dick Geary undertook his first mission on 4 October. Both sorties were uneventful.

Another Mosquito unit to boast USAAF crews was No 157 Sqn, which had moved to Predannack, in Cornwall, in early November for operations over the Bay of Biscay. On the 19th, a formation set out on an 'Instep' patrol to intercept Fw 200s and Bv 222s operating from Bordeaux/Merignac. In the formation were Lts McDonald and Barron, attached from the USAAF, but their Mosquito developed an engine problem and ditched, breaking in two. One of the Americans was seen clinging to the wreckage but neither was recovered. It was only their second operational sortie.

Earlier in the summer the RCAF's specialist night intruder unit, No 418 Sqn, which was in the process of exchanging its Bostons for more effective Mosquito FB VIs, received an experienced American-born CO in the shape of Wg Cdr Paul Davoud. Upon his return to operations he immediately won his crews' respect, being described by future seven-victory ace Don MacFadyen as;

'A convincing leader who inspired people by consistency of personal behaviour, he used human resources creatively, and knew how to deal with a gaggle of strong-willed fellows coming fresh to the night intruding business. He knew how to fly too, and set the example with proper airmanship. It was very much to Paul's credit that No 418 Sqn became so effective.'

One of Davoud's first operations in this new role came on 12 July when he attacked French rail traffic. Two nights later he raided Rennes airfield. A period of fine weather in early August increased the opportunities for intruder sorties, and on the 7th Davoud visited St Dizier. He reported seeing two large bursts in the administration site caused by his bombs. Another of his compatriots who arrived on the squadron on 8 September was 1Lt James Luma from Montana. Having originally joined the RCAF and trained for intruder duties, he was transferred to the USAAF, but found himself back with the RCAF because of his specialist training.

No 605 Sqn at Bradwell Bay also received a complement of Americans at this time, starting with the arrival of Flt Off 'Bud' Miller, a non-commissioned USAAF pilot who joined 'B' Flight. The squadron diary noted that he and his navigator, Flg Off Winlaw, 'both became very popular, and during their tour they destroyed one enemy aircraft,

One of the first Mosquito II units to have USAAF aircrew attached to it was No 157 Sqn, although its first crew was lost on 19 November 1943 during a sortie over the Bay of Biscay while hunting for enemy long-range bombers (*F G Swanborough*)

In mid-1943, Wg Cdr Paul Davoud (closest to the camera) returned to operations as CO of Mosquito FB VI-equipped No 418 Sqn, which was tasked with performing intruder duties. Squadron personnel included several successful American-born pilots serving in both the USAAF and RCAF (*PAC*)

damaged three and destroyed a "diver". "Bud's" rank, Flight Officer, has no real equivalent in the RAF, it being a sort of commissioned Warrant Officer, and he was granted this rank when he transferred to the USAAF from the RAF, where he had been intending to join one of the "Eagle" squadrons. Not only were they a very useful operational crew but the squadron blessed them for the good they did on the welfare side.'

The new crew made their operational debut on 10 November. They were up again the following night, as the unit's diary noted;

'"Bud" plodded round and round the 'drome dodging the flak, and came back wondering whether intruding was quite the thing, and as attractive as he had thought. He soon learned, however, and later was to go in and beat up the 'drome without getting hit.'

THE 'BABY *BLITZ*'

Late in November fellow non-commissioned USAAF pilot TSgt V J Chipman was also posted to No 605 Sqn, and he duly flew his first operational mission to the Frisian Islands before the month was out. On 4 January 1944, fellow American pilot, albeit one serving in the RCAF, Flt Lt Glen Holland flew his first sortie to Dreux. That same night 'Bud' Miller visited Laon, where he spotted a twin-engined aircraft taking off at Roye. Although he bombed the airfield, he lost contact with the aircraft.

Flt Off 'Bud' Miller is pictured (left) standing in front of Mosquito FB VI HX823/UP-K with his navigator. This was his regular aircraft for a time while he was with No 605 Sqn, and it was flown by another successful American pilot, Flt Lt Glen Holland. The latter was flying it on 15 March 1944 when he shot up some locomotives in the Ansbach area (*No 605 Squadron records*)

The nose of this No 605 Sqn Mosquito displays the score achieved by its usual pilot, ace Flt Lt David Blomeley, although it was also flown by two of the squadron's USAAF pilots. On one of the first sorties of 1944, TSgt V J Chipman flew it on an intruder mission to the nightfighter base at St Trond, in Belgium (*via B Cull*)

The Mosquito FB VI intruders of No 418 Sqn caused considerable damage to the enemy during 1944. Many of the unit's pilots, including several Americans, saw action during this period (*P H T Green Collection*)

While flying No 410 Sqn Mosquito XIII HK429/RA-N on the night of 3 February 1944, USAAF pilot Flt Off Dick Geary almost had a mid-air collision with an Fw 190 near London. The aircraft was also occasionally flown by 1Lt Archie Harrington (*Canadian Forces*)

Canadian ace Flg Off Rayne Schultz demonstrates to his No 410 Sqn colleague Flt Off Dick Geary (right) how he shot down three enemy bombers in December 1943 (*V A Williams*)

By late 1943 a number of USAAF pilots were attached to RCAF Mosquito nightfighter unit No 410 Sqn. Among them was 1Lt Archie Harrington, who flew Mosquito XIII HK430/RA-V several times during the 'Baby *Blitz*' of early 1944 (*Canadian Forces*)

An American who was to become a successful intruder pilot with No 418 Sqn was Flg Off Murl Jasper. The 28-year-old Kansan had also previously been an instructor, prior to arriving in the frontline at the turn of the year. Jasper's new aircraft made an immediate impression on him, as he later recalled;

'The Mosquito was beautiful! It was tricky as hell on take-off and landing. You had very little rudder control to begin with on take-off. When you opened the throttles, you opened them gingerly and used them for directional control, but once the tail got off the ground, you could use the rudder controls pretty well. The Mosquito was very light on the controls once you got it in the air. It was manoeuvrable as hell, but it wouldn't turn with a single-engined fighter. Of course we could outrun a '109 or '190 as long as it didn't have an altitude advantage.'

No 410 Sqn's American pilots continued flying on operations into the winter of 1943/44, with Archie Harrington beginning what was to be a fruitful partnership with his new navigator, Sgt Dennis Tongue. As the winter progressed, the Luftwaffe began the series of attacks on Britain that became known as the 'Baby *Blitz*'. It was to generate plenty of 'trade' for the defending nightfighter crews.

Shortly before midnight on 3 January, Flt Off Dick Geary gained a contact in the Bradwell Bay area, which he chased to the edge of the London anti-aircraft gun zone. There, to his intense frustration, he was called off.

Geary had a narrow escape early the following month when flying Mosquito XIII HK429/RA-N. He

gained a visual on an Fw 190 but narrowly avoided colliding with it head-on as it passed his aircraft. Five nights later, on 8 February, No 410 Sqn flew no fewer than 18 patrols, of which six had been scrambles. Five radar contacts and four visuals were gained. Geary left soon afterwards, leaving Archie Harrington as the sole USAAF pilot still serving with No 410 Sqn. It was not long before he was joined by another American pilot serving with the RCAF, however.

Like Harrington, 28-year-old Flt Lt Charles 'Pop' Edinger from Onaway, Michigan, had previously served as a flying instructor, but was soon to establish himself as one of No 410 Sqn's leading pilots. It was Harrington, however, who was the first American to be blooded with the unit. Returning to base after an uneventful scramble late on 14 March, he and his navigator, Dennis Tongue, saw some incendiaries, bomb bursts and searchlight beams. Although short of fuel, they proceeded to investigate and obtained a radar contact. In spite of skilful evasive action by the German pilot, Tongue retained contact, enabling Harrington to identify a Ju 188. In his combat report the American pilot wrote;

1Lt Archie Harrington from Janesville, Ohio, ended the war with seven victories to his name, making him jointly the most successful American nightfighter pilot of the war (*V A Williams*)

'I closed to 100 ft (30 m) from dead astern and slightly below. I fired a short burst with slight deflections from 100 ft to 150 ft. Strikes were clearly observed on the cockpit and wing roots. Instantly, we saw a red glow in cockpit itself, almost immediately followed by both engines bursting into flames. This developed and enveloped the whole area between the engines, including the cockpit, streaming back in a solid sheet of flame two to three times the enemy aircraft's length.'

In claiming the first night victory for a USAAF pilot flying with the RCAF, Archie Harrington had fired just 35 rounds from his cannon.

The intruders also remained active, and in the early hours of 22 January, No 418 Sqn's 'Lou' Luma was flying near Wunstorf when two bright lights were seen. He wrote afterwards;

'We did a quick orbit to port, coming behind him and chasing him for about 15-20 miles (24-30 km). We were on his tail and gave him a 2-3 second burst of cannon and machine guns from about 250 yrd (230 m) down to 100 yrd (90 m), pulling up from about 500 ft below to practically on top of him. Strikes on the fuselage were followed by a ball of fire, which enabled us to identify the enemy aircraft as an Me 410. A large piece broke off to the left and it went down, exploding and burning on the ground.'

When he returned from this sortie, Luma found two pieces of his victim embedded in the wing of his Mosquito.

Although he had lived in Canada before the war and enlisted in the RCAF, 24-year-old Flg Off Tom Anderson had been born in Fargo,

North Dakota. Having initially served as an instructor, he too eventually found himself flying operations with No 418 Sqn. On the night of 3 February he flew an eventful 'Ranger' to Tours. The squadron's operations diary noted;

'He saw one enemy aircraft with lights landing. He orbited and saw a second enemy aircraft with lights approaching. Turning in, he followed exhaust flames and identified the contact as a twin-engined type. From 400 yrd down to 200 yrd (185 m), he gave him a three-second burst. Strikes were seen all over the fuselage. Light flak followed from the nearby airfield, so he broke to port and saw the enemy aircraft burning on the ground – flames could still be seen when 20 miles (32 km) away.'

His countryman, 'Lou' Luma, continued to see action too. In the early hours of 13 February, with his navigator Flg Off Colin Finlayson, he was in the Bordeaux area hunting the long-range bombers that were harassing shipping convoys in the Atlantic. Just before 0200 hrs the crew spotted the lights of an aircraft following them, as Luma himself described;

'We recognised him in the bright moonlight as an He 177. As he passed over the beacon, he doused the navigation lights, leaving just the tail lights on. We gave him a two-second burst of cannon and machine guns from 150 yrd down to 100yrd (140 m to 90 m) from below and astern. We were then at 1300 ft (400 m), and saw that he had his wheels down. There was an explosion in the region of the cockpit and, as we shot under him, he appeared to be diving down after us. We broke off to starboard and the enemy aircraft went straight in three miles (5 km) south of Bordeaux. He exploded with brilliant white sparks and was burning as we left.'

The 21-year-old had taken his next step to becoming an ace.

The Americans in No 605 Sqn also continued to harass the enemy in his own backyard, with Miller flying a 'Flower' bomber-support sortie on 19 February to Parleburg, where he attacked a taxiing aircraft. The following night, Chipman was in the Handorf area, where, at just after 0500 hrs, he spotted an aircraft. He was perfectly positioned and opened fire from 100 yrd, as he reported afterwards;

'I saw strikes along the fuselage and on the starboard wing between the fuselage and the engine nacelle. A blinding flash soon followed, and by the light of this I recognised it as probably being a Ju 88. The explosion caused the wing section to be lifted, and in my opinion the starboard wing looked untrue as I broke off the attack.'

Chipman experienced some flak while claiming his first scalp. Not to be outdone, Flt Off 'Bud' Miller destroyed an aircraft at Brussels/Melsbroek during an intruder sortie on the 23rd. He had claimed his first victory, as he recalled later;

'At 0145 hrs we observed an aircraft with its navigation lights on taxiing along the perimeter track. We opened fire from 400 ft (120 m) and continued firing down to a

Included in No 418 Sqn's contingent of American personnel was 1Lt 'Lou' Luma, a USAAF pilot on secondment to the RCAF. He and his regular navigator, Flg Off Colin Finlayson (to rear), are seen here surveying the damage to the fin of their Mosquito after an eventful intruder mission (*Canadian Forces*)

height of just 150 ft. We observed strikes and the enemy aircraft caught fire. It burned for 20 minutes. From the wingspan I would say it was a twin-engined aircraft.'

The following night, in clear, starry weather, Flt Lt Glen Holland also flew an intruder sortie to the Brussels area where he damaged an unidentified aircraft. It was the first of the 25-year-old's five claims with No 605 Sqn. The next night he was over Germany, where he caught a Bf 110 nightfighter near Ansbach. Holland subsequently reported;

'We had passed the runway when we saw an enemy aircraft's landing lights approaching to land. They were flicked on and off several times. We turned back to try and get into position to attack the enemy aircraft on the runway, but were unable to manoeuvre whilst its lights were on. We turned and attacked from the southwest, opening fire at a height of about 100 ft and a range of approximately 200 yrd. Strikes were seen to the rear of the cockpit, crossing through to the port engine and into the hangar. The enemy aircraft was recognised as a Me 110 in the lights of the hangar. We broke away to port to avoid the hangar and other obstructions.'

He then continued with the sortie, attacking several trains that were seen in marshalling yards, before heading for home.

The intruder units remained busy in March, with Chipman, who was now a Flight Officer, having an encounter near Paris in the early hours of the 2nd;

'I did a very tight diving turn to get my sights on him, opening fire with a medium burst at approximately 200 ft range above and to port as the enemy aircraft was touching down. Many strikes were seen moving from the port wing through to the cockpit and along the starboard wing. In the light of the strikes I recognised two inline engines and a long "glasshouse" cockpit cover – probably an Me 110.'

A few nights later, on the evening of the 6th, Luma and Finlayson of No 418 Sqn destroyed an Fw 190 at Pau during a 'Ranger' to Clermont. Their Mosquito was, however, struck by debris from their victim as it exploded, and the pair flew back 600 miles (960 km) on one engine. Luma later said it had been 'a shaky do'.

It was during a 'Day Ranger' mission that Luma's squadron colleague, Murl Jasper (with navigator Flt Lt Archie Martin) made his first claim. Flying as No 2 to future ace Flt Lt John Caine, Jasper vividly recalled;

'When we hit the 'drome, Johnny set one aeroplane on the ground on fire. I just damaged one – a twin-engine Ju 86P. We hit the field just once and kept heading north for home. Archie looked back and spotted an Fw 190 diving on our tails. He had altitude and speed on us. I radioed Johnny. When the Focke-Wulf got to within 400-500 yrds (370-460 m) of our tail, Johnny hollered "Break right!" I broke right. He broke left and came around, trying to get on the German's tail. The '190 got the idea

Standing in front of Mosquito VI HJ719/TH-U MOONBEAM McSWINE on 3 April 1944 are two of No 418 Sqn's outstanding intruder crews. They are, from left to right, Sqn Ldr Howie Cleveland and his navigator Flt Sgt Frank Day, and 1Lt James Luma (USAAF on secondment) and his navigator Flg Off Colin Finlayson. Both the pilots had recently become aces, with Luma achieving this distinction on 21 March when, during an attack on Luxeuil airfield, he shot down two enemy aircraft, destroyed two more on the ground and damaged four others (Canadian Forces)

that it wasn't a healthy place to be and chandelled out of there. We hightailed it for home.'

A week later Flt Lt Holland flew to Rheine, where he spotted a Ju 88;

'A 2-3 second burst was fired and a good concentration of strikes was seen. We passed over it, turned to the right and saw flames and a small explosion. We turned downwind on the north side of the aerodrome and the Ju 88 was seen to be still burning.'

Four nights after his second victory, Glen Holland took off for an intruder mission to the nightfighter training base at Schleissheim. Nothing was seen until he and his navigator reached Neuberg, midway between Nuremberg and Munich. The airfield was found to be fully lit. After investigating several possibilities, they spotted an Fw 190 in the circuit, which they promptly shot down. This was closely followed by the destruction of another enemy aircraft which the pair was unable to identify. Glen Holland wrote immediately afterwards;

'I closed to approximately 150 yrd, recognising him as an Fw 190, and I gave him a two-second burst. Strikes were seen and he erupted in flames. I did a quick turn to starboard to avoid hitting him and he did a slow spiral dive into the ground, exploding and burning on impact. I returned to Neuburg at 2303 hrs. It was still lit, and I saw an aircraft approaching to land with its navigation lights on. It landed to the left of the main runway. I closed to 100 yrd at about 50 ft (15 m) height, recognising the enemy aircraft as being single-engined. I gave him a one-second burst, and he exploded immediately and burst into flames. I turned back and took a cine shot of the wreckage, then set course for base.'

These victories took his total to four destroyed and one damaged. But Glen Holland was destined not to become an ace, for on the night of 20/21 April 1944, he and navigator Flg Off W H Wilkinson failed to return from an intruder mission to Rheine.

Two evenings before Holland's final success on 23/24 March, 'Lou' Luma, together with future RCAF ace Don MacFadyen, flew an intruder mission to Luxeuil. Nearing the airfield at just after 1800 hrs, the young American shot down an ancient Junkers W 34 liaison aircraft. Fifteen minutes later he caught a Ju 52/3m transport to claim his fifth, and final, victory. Luma had now become the USAAF's first nightfighter ace.

Murl Jasper gained his first victory on 12 April when, near Verdun, his navigator, Archie Martin, spotted a light. They investigated and closed on an Fw 190. Their devastating fire causing the enemy fighter to break up and crash. Four nights later Jasper joined three other Mosquitoes for a 'Day Ranger' mission to Luxeuil, in eastern France. There, the Kansan spotted several French-built Caudron Goeland twin-engined transports about to take-off, as he reported;

'When I came across the 'drome, I lined up on two Goelands. I could see that one was loading troops, and I splattered the hell out of them. One caught fire and blew up. I flew over and found one transport taxiing out. It apparently had already loaded up. I blew him up. Over the runway, I found another Goeland that had just taken off and was 300 ft (90 m) in the air. I pulled in behind him. He exploded when he hit the ground.'

Nearly a month later, on 14 May, Jasper achieved his third success during a 'Day Ranger' to eastern France that was flown in heavy rain and low cloud. He reported;

'It was right near Strasbourg that this He 111 came barrelling out of the rain right at me. It was damn near a head-on collision! I passed him going in the opposite direction, so I did a 90-degree turnaround. If I'd done a 180, I wouldn't have found him. So I did a 90 and came around. Pretty soon he showed up in the rain. I was closing on him pretty fast, and damn near ran into him. At 50 yrd (46 m) I gave him about a half-second burst. Fortunately, at that range, he didn't blow up. His left engine just went up and then I lost him. I tried to find him again but never did. The wreck was found later and Fighter Command confirmed the kill.'

Later in the sortie Jasper destroyed a Ju 87 on the ground at Azelot.

While the intruder units had been busy, the end of the so-called 'Baby Blitz' reduced the opportunities for the defensive nightfighter crews. With the invasion of France imminent, however, nightfighter crews were trained to a peak of effectiveness to defend the vulnerable landing forces when the time came. 'Pop' Edinger eventually began operations with No 410 Sqn on 3 May when he flew an uneventful patrol accompanied by Flg Off Vaesson, with whom he was soon to build a successful career.

D-DAY DEFENDERS

June began promisingly for No 418 Sqn's Americans. They continued their run of success when Tom Anderson shot down a Do 17 over Plan de Dieu on the 1st. Four days later, a four-aircraft detachment from No 410 Sqn went to Colerne to provide nightfighter cover for the initial airborne landings which preceded the invasion that night. One of the pilots was 'Pop' Edinger. Meanwhile, back at Hunsdon, ten more Mosquitoes were at readiness, although all patrols proved uneventful. On the nights immediately following the landings, No 410 Sqn flew further patrols to cover the invasion fleet and the landing beaches.

Hazards came not just from the enemy, as Archie Harrington found during the early hours of the 8th. As he closed on an aircraft, which he identified as being a Lancaster, its rear gunner opened fire – Allied bomber crews were taking no chances.

Very bad weather precluded operations for several nights, but on the evening of 12 June No 410 Sqn's Mosquitoes were again over the expanding beachhead to counter the increasingly heavy enemy attacks. Most contacts turned out to be friendly aircraft, but in the early hours of the 14th Edinger, who was 'freelancing' with radio failure, attacked and damaged a Ju 88 in his first combat. Four nights later he took the first step towards becoming an ace. He described this momentous event in his combat report;

'I obtained a visual and identified it as a Ju 188. I closed to 100 yrd (90 m) to check its identity and then opened fire. my first burst over-deflected and missed in front, but my second burst struck the port wing and engine nacelle. The enemy aircraft spun into the sea and exploded.'

Returning to base, Edinger spot-ted a 'pilotless aircraft' over the

These Mosquito NF XXXs of No 410 Sqn await their next sorties at B 48 Amiens/Glisy during the autumn of 1944. The nearest aircraft is MM788/RA-Q, which was flown on occasion by American six-victory ace Flt Lt 'Pop' Edinger. Indeed, he used the fighter to fly an uneventful patrol over Nijmegen on the evening of 18 October (*D Tongue*)

Thames Estuary. He gave chase and fired, but saw no result. No 410 Sqn had experienced its first encounter with a V1 flying bomb. Later that day Harrington and Sgt Tongue were over the area of the American landings near Vire, as Archie Harrington's combat report noted;

'We were vectored and contact was obtained at a range of three miles (4.8 km). When approximately one mile away, the contact proved to be two aircraft, one of which broke to port and the other to starboard. We followed the aircraft going to port through a hard port turn. We closed in to 400 ft (120m) and identified it as a Ju 88 carrying two large bombs. We closed in to 200 ft (60 m), pulled the nose up and opened fire from below. Closing in to 75 ft (20 m), we finished the attack from slightly above. No strikes were observed until quite suddenly the aircraft exploded in the air. The engine and port wing broke off and went by us on our port side. Masses of debris and burning oil came back, striking our aircraft.'

THE 'BUZZ-BOMB' SUMMER

With the opening of the German V1 flying bomb offensive against southern England, the Mosquito units regularly began encountering these small but dangerous targets. On the night of 19 June, Merl Jasper is thought to have become the first American nightfighter pilot to down a V1 – his first of three. Two nights later, No 605 Sqn's 'Bud' Miller followed suit, taking his first step towards becoming the USAAF's sole V1 ace. But it was also his swansong, for soon afterwards he was transferred to the Tempest Flight of the elite FIU at Newchurch for experimental nightfighting work.

It was towards the end of the month that Jasper downed his final enemy aircraft. Flying over the Baltic just north of Rostock on 27 June, he spotted a Ju 88, but was still able to notice a festive-looking Ferris wheel near the town! In his report, he described how he worked his way behind the bomber;

'We then opened fire with a two-second burst of cannon and machine gun from 150 yrd (140 m), closing to 50 yrd (45 m). Strikes were seen on both wing roots. The port engine burst into flames, followed almost immediately by the starboard. A violent explosion then took place. The Ju 88 disintegrated and flaming pieces fell into the sea over a wide area. We then pulled away to starboard, but even so, our aircraft sustained slight damage in that the fabric on the rudder was almost entirely burned off, as was a large strip of fabric on the port side of the fuselage and a smaller piece of the port wing.'

The Americans in No 410 Sqn also remained active. On 3 July 'Pop' Edinger was successful once more when he attacked a bomber northeast of Pointe et Raz. He reported;

'We closed in and recognised a Ju 188, then dropped below and dead astern. The enemy aircraft peeled off violently to port as though he had seen us. We followed the peel-off visually and fired a short burst. Strikes were seen on the port nacelle, and the port wing was seen to blow off. The nacelle was burning fiercely and the enemy aircraft spun into the sea.'

At the end of July the FIU's Tempest V EJ535 had been fitted with Monica IIIE radar equipment for evaluation against the flying bombs. 'Bud' Miller flew the Tempest for the first time on 3 August, although in the last ten days of July he had destroyed two V1s with a standard aircraft.

Although of indifferent quality, this is one of the few photographs of USAAF V1 ace Flt Off 'Bud' Miller of No 501 Sqn (*P H T Green collection*)

In early August the Tempest Flight was transferred to No 501 Sqn to instruct the unit on how to perform the 'anti-diver' night interception mission. At 1100 hrs on 11 August Miller took off in Tempest V EJ584/SD-Q, as he described afterwards;

'I was patrolling under Watling control. The first "diver" was seen coming from the southwest at 1000 ft (300 m) and 350 mph (560 km/h). I fired three two-second bursts from 50 yrd and saw pieces fall off. The "diver" went down and crashed eight miles (13 km) east of Tonbridge. The second "diver" was at same height and speed as the first. I fired from 100 yrd astern. The "Diver" crashed and exploded a few miles northeast of Tonbridge.'

Miller continued his patrol, destroying a third V1 near Sandwich. He shot down two more flying bombs soon after dawn on 16 September and on the night of the 24th made his final claim when, at the controls of Tempest V EJ558/SD-R, he brought down his ninth flying bomb as it was crossing the coast near Bradwell Bay. It had been launched by an He 111H-20 over the North Sea.

Once airfields had been secured after the Normandy invasion the nightfighter squadrons of the 2nd Tactical Air Force, including No 410 Sqn, began to move to the Continent. Initially, however, the squadron remained at Hunsdon, and it was from here that Flt Lt 'Pop' Edinger, accompanied by Chuck Vaessen, left to patrol the Antwerp area early on 17 September. The Mosquito was then vectored northeast in pursuit of a contact. Despite the unidentified bogey's violent evasive manoeuvres, the Mosquito chased it until it entered a high-speed stall and crashed from low level. 'Pop' Edinger had not fired a single shot to achieve his third victory, and his squadron's 50th.

On 22 September No 410 Sqn moved to airfield B 48 Amiens/Glisy, from where three patrols were flown over the battle area that very day. On the evening of the 26th Archie Harrington took off to patrol the frontline, and at 2130 hrs he was directed to a contact flying at low level. He managed to close in and identify it as a Ju 87, as he reported later;

'I then dropped back to approximately 300 ft (90 m) and opened fire. Strikes were observed on the wing root and fuselage, and the enemy

Tempest V EJ558/SD-R of No 501 Sqn is seen here taxiing at Bradwell Bay on 15 October 1944. It latterly was the usual mount of Flt Off 'Bud' Miller, whose impressive V1 kill 'log' is displayed below the cockpit. With nine flying bombs destroyed, Miller is almost certainly the only USAAF pilot to have become a V1 ace (*via C H Thomas*)

aircraft's undercarriage was blown off. It then turned slowly to starboard and lost height. Meanwhile, the rear gunner fired a Very signal. I believe that the pilot was killed outright in this first burst because of the nature of the turn. We followed the aircraft around, and gave it two additional bursts. Strikes were observed all over the fuselage, which, however, refused to catch fire. The enemy aircraft passed under my wing and exploded violently on the ground, where it was seen burning very nicely.'

It was Harrington's third success.

During the evening of 6 October, Edinger and Vaessen were on patrol northeast of Namur. No 410 Sqn's history vividly described what happened next;

'"Pop" and Chuck were vectored south after some "trade" 30 miles (48 km) distant. Closing in, Edinger recognised it as a Ju 88, and with one short burst he set fire to the port engine and turned to one side to watch developments. But the fire died out and for a moment the Junkers disappeared. Hurriedly nosing down, the Mosquito closed on it until the quarry again came in view, going down in a series of hard orbits to port. Edinger cut in once more for a long burst that caused both engines to blaze. Rolling to one side, the Ju 88 went straight in, exploding as it crashed 16 miles (26 km) from Namur, where the wreckage was found by a ground party.'

As a result of gaining his fourth victory, the 28-year-old from Michigan received the DFC.

The rest of the October nights passed relatively uneventfully, except for occasional sightings of V2 rockets being launched against England. However, on the afternoon of the 29th, Archie Harrington and Dennis Tongue claimed another scalp after a long chase over eastern Holland. Eventually they closed in for the kill, as the combat report stated;

'A positive identification was made on an Fw 190 with the aid of night binoculars. I closed in to approximately 150 ft (46 m) and fired. Strikes were seen around the cockpit, and it shed various debris and went into a port spiral dive. Another burst was fired at about 100 ft (30 m) – more strikes on the cockpit. Two more bursts were given at approximately 30-40 ft (9-12 m) range, whereupon the enemy aircraft turned on its back and plunged vertically into the ground, where it burned fiercely.'

The RAF's nightfighting expertise received further American recognition with the attachment of five US Navy crews to Nos 68 and 456 Sqns. The objective was to gain experience with these veteran units as the US Navy embarked on its own nightfighter programme. The first personnel to fly an operational sortie with No 456 Sqn were Lt Cdrs Sinclair and Gould in Mosquito XIII HK297 in the early hours of 30 October. They were followed soon afterwards by Lt Woodward and Ens Madden.

The three Navy crews attached to No 68 Sqn began operations on the 22nd when Lt Peebles and his navigator Lt Grinndal flew an 'anti-diver' patrol. But the US Navy's

During the autumn of 1944 a number of US Navy crews were attached to fly Mosquito XVIIs with Nos 68 and 456 Sqns from their bases in East Anglia. One of the latter unit's aircraft was HK312/RX-G. Three of the five crews were lost during their brief attachment (J W Bennett)

exposure to nightfighter operations with the RAF was to result in tragedy. On 7 November 'Woody' Woodward and 'Jerry' Madden took off to fly a defensive patrol in the Arnhem area. The weather was bad with heavy rain and gale-force winds that were so high that Brighton Pier was blown down. The unit's diary noted dryly that 'it is regretted that Lt Woodward and Ens Madden, who took off from Ford, did not return'.

Worse was to follow a week later when a No 68 Sqn Mosquito left Coltishall to counter air-launched V1 flying bombs. Having apparently found one of the missiles near Lowestoft, the aircraft's crew followed it into an anti-aircraft gun zone instead of chasing the He 111 'mother-ship'. The Mosquito was engaged by friendly anti-aircraft guns and set on fire. Lts Black and Aitken were killed when it crashed. Then, on the 22nd, No 68 Sqn lost another US Navy crew when Lts Peebles and Grinndal crashed shortly after take-off and died in the subsequent crash. The surviving crews completed their attachment at the end of the month and returned to the US.

A NIGHT TO REMEMBER

Meanwhile, in France, No 410 Sqn had moved to B 51 at Lille/Vendeville on 3 November. Early on the evening of the 25th, Harrington and Tongue left the airfield in Mosquito NF XXX MM767/RA-O for another night-fighter patrol over Germany. The first hour of their sortie, under the control of a mobile radar unit with the call-sign of 'Bricktile', was uneventful. They were then handed over to another unit and vectored towards a contact. Archie Harrington subsequently reported;

'Visual contact obtained at 4500 ft (1400 m), height 16,000 ft (5000 m). I closed right in and finally identified it as Ju 88 nightfighter with a Ju 188 tail. It had Ju 88G-1 blister under the nose, black crosses clearly seen on the wings and radar aerials clearly seen projecting from the nose. I dropped back to approximately 600 ft (185 m) and opened fire. Strikes were seen in the cockpit, engines and wing roots, followed by explosion and debris. The enemy aircraft dived very steeply, and I followed it on AI and visually. I saw the Ju 88 strike the ground and burst into flames.'

The Mosquito had, however, been hit by debris, causing some vibration. In claiming his all-important fifth victory, and with it elevation to ace status, Harrington had shot down Ju 88G-1 Wk-Nr 712295 of 4./NJG 4. The aircraft had been flown by ex-bomber pilot Hauptmann Erwin Strobel, who, with his radar operator, Unteroffizier Horst Scheitzke, and gunner, Unteroffizier Otto Palme, managed

One of No 410 Sqn's star pilots was 1Lt Archie Harrington, who became an ace in spectacular style on the night of 25 November 1944 when he and his navigator, Flg Off Dennis Tongue, shot down three Ju 88 nightfighters. He is pictured here with Plt Off Keeping (*V A Williams*)

Harrington's aircraft on 25 November was Mosquito NF XXX MM767/RA-O, which is seen here still displaying the remnants of its black and white AEAF stripes under the fuselage. Harrington had also flown the aircraft to claim his fourth victory on 29 October, when he shot down an Fw 190 over Belgium (*Canadian Forces*)

to bale out of the stricken aircraft just moments prior to crashing near Geisenkirchen.

Almost immediately Dennis Tongue obtained a head-on contact, although the target appeared to be trying to intercept the Mosquito. This cat and mouse game continued for ten minutes before the Mosquito closed in on the tail of Leutnant Fensch's 5./NJG 4 Ju 88G. The latter was hit and stalled before crashing. Harrington and Tongue were then vectored onto a further pair of hostiles three miles (2.8 km) away. They selected the port contact, with Tongue watching the tail as the second aircraft appeared to be trying to intercept them – with so many enemy nightfighters around they could afford to take no chances. Harrington described the final stages of the engagement in his combat report;

'We closed in and identified it as a Ju 88, with a Ju 188 tail. Still doing evasive action, it suddenly throttled back and I narrowly escaped ramming him. Then I dropped back 300 ft and opened fire. Strikes were seen in the cockpit, on the engines and the wing roots. Debris flew off, and the aircraft's port engine then started burning. Fire spread to the cockpit and starboard engine, and the aircraft went down in a spiral dive to starboard. I followed, taking pictures of it burning. It went into cloud, and a few seconds later a very large explosion lit up the underside of the target, which continued to burn fiercely.'

Ju 88G Wk-Nr 714508 of 3./NJG 4 had become Harrington's third victim. The No 410 Sqn records succinctly summarised the events – 'Take-off 1740 hrs, landed 2115 hrs. Three contacts, three visual, three combats, three Ju 88s destroyed.'

This eventful 18-minute period resulted in Archie Harrington being credited with three enemy aircraft destroyed in what is thought to have been the most successful night's combat by a USAAF pilot in World War 2. It took his final score to seven, making him the joint leading USAAF nightfighter pilot of the conflict. Both pilot and navigator had previously been recommended for the DFC, and as a result of this action, Harrington received a DSO and Tongue a bar to his DFC.

On the night of Harrington's success, another USAAF pilot serving with a British squadron was also flying over Germany in a Mosquito. Flt Off R D S Gregor, usually known as 'Hank', was serving with No 141 Sqn in the bomber-support role. That night he was flying an intruder mission against enemy airfields.

As 1944 came to an end, bad weather greatly interfered with operations and enabled the Germans to prepare for a surprise offensive in the Ardennes, which opened on 16 December. Two days later, 'Pop' Edinger and Chuck Vaessen were airborne over the Nijmegen area, the pilot suspecting that they might be lucky as he had always made a claim just before going on leave. His intuition was not misplaced, for after tracking a violently-manoeuvring target, they closed in. Erdinger subsequently reported;

The final victory scored by a USAAF nightfighter pilot serving with the RAF in World War 2 was claimed on 14 March 1945 by 2Lt 'Hank' Gregor (right) of No 141 Sqn, who is seen here with his navigator, Flt Sgt Frank Baker (*via M Bowman*)

'We identified it as a Ju 88. The aircraft continued hard evasion for several minutes, and I was unable to bring my guns to bear. Finally, it went into a steep turn to starboard and I fired a short burst, scoring strikes on the starboard engine and fuselage and starting a small fire in the starboard engine. The turn steepened, and it went down under my starboard wing. We were unable to follow as we were very low – approximately 200 ft (60 m). My navigator could see the trees. We did a climbing turn to starboard and it was seen to hit the ground and explode.'

This was the American's fifth victory, admitting him to the elite band of nightfighter aces. He was also the last US nightfighter pilot to become an ace while serving with the British and Commonwealth forces. It was not his final fling, however, as the No 410 Sqn records point out;

'"Pop" and Chuck were the first crew off on Christmas Eve, leaving Vendeville to patrol the Dutch border between Sittard and Venlo. Then control put them onto a "bogey". Closing within sight of the enemy, now recognised as a Ju 87, Edinger had to lower his flaps and undercarriage to reduce speed to that of the slow-moving Stuka. His first burst resulted in debris from wings and fuselage, and a second burst, at closer range, yielded more fragments, but still no fire. Again he fired, and this time the Ju 87 burst into flames as it dived toward the ground. Oddly, the enemy pilot took no evasive action during the combat. The location was near Wassenberg, southeast of Roermond.'

It was Edinger's final success, and in the early weeks of 1945, No 410 Sqn's Americans gradually left at the end of their very productive and successful tours. Edinger's was, however, not the last victory by an American flying nightfighters with the RAF. On the night of 14 March 2Lt Hank Gregor and his navigator, Flt Sgt Frank Baker, flying in a Mosquito FB VI, were operating in support of a Bomber Command night raid on Zweibrucken. In the Frankfurt-Mannheim area, the pair spotted an aircraft approaching to land. Closing in quickly, they opened fire and the enemy nightfighter exploded, lighting up the sky. Having claimed No 141 Sqn's 70th, and last, victory of the war, Gregor wrote;

'I opened fire at the silver shape, spraying the area. We rapidly closed range to 100 ft (30 m), and just as we started to pull out, the enemy aircraft exploded under our nose, illuminating the area. Almost immediately light flak, not too accurate, came up at us, and a searchlight conned us. I hooked back on the stick and we left for home.'

YANKS IN BEAUS

By mid-1942, RAF strike and nightfighter Beaufighter squadrons were based both in Egypt and on Malta. Among the reinforcements sent to the latter island in the summer of 1942 was a detachment of Beaufighters from No 235 Sqn, which, on 20 August, became independent operating from Luqa as No 227 Sqn. Shortly afterwards, the enemy commenced the Battle of Alam Halfa in North Africa, this three-pronged strike proving to be the *Afrika Korps'* final offensive. In spite of many deprivations, the Malta-based strike squadrons were kept busy interdicting the enemy's supply routes across the Mediterranean.

The pressure was maintained into September, when 32-year-old Flg Off Carl Johnson from Banks, Oregon, joined No 227 Sqn. He flew his first operation on the 25th, but the Beaufighters failed to find the warship that had been reported off the Tunisian port of Sfax. Off Kuriat Island, however, they spotted Cant Z.506B flying boat MM45435 of 197ᵃ *Squadriglia*. Flown by Mar Pil Attilio Broccaro, the aircraft was conducting an air-sea rescue search. The Beaufighters immediately attacked, sending the hapless flying boat crashing into the Mediterranean. It was then strafed and destroyed, although its wounded pilot and three others were later rescued. For Carl Johnson, it was his first step to becoming an ace.

Johnson flew shipping strikes almost daily, and with the opening of the decisive Battle of El Alamein on 23 October, the denial of supplies, particularly fuel, to the enemy increased in importance. No 227 Sqn was reinforced in early November by 272 Sqn, which had a successful day on the 12th. Twenty-four hours later it was No 227 Sqn's turn when a

A Beaufighter VIC of No 227 Sqn lifts off from Malta soon after the unit had formed in August 1942. It was heavily involved in attacks on enemy air and sea transport and sustained correspondingly heavy losses. One of the squadron's leading pilots was Flt Lt Carl Johnson, an American serving with the RAF. He achieved four victories plus one shared before being killed in action (*via J D Oughton*)

Do 24 flying boat and six Ju 52/3m and SM.81 transports were shot down off the Tunisian coast. However, on the 14th No 227 Sqn's attack on the enemy base at Bizerte was less successful. As the formation flew over some enemy warships, their escorting fighters promptly attacked the Beaufighters. They headed rapidly for cloud cover but not before two had been shot down, one of them by a Bf 109 flown by Unteroffizier Hartmut Klotzer of III./JG 53. But the German pilot did not have long to savour his success, for Carl Johnson promptly shot him down into the sea.

Later that same day, the American, who was flying EL232/J, followed up this rare victory over such a dangerous adversary by shooting down a Ju 88 of 1(F)./122 that was on a reconnaissance mission. No 227 Sqn's mission log noted that, '"J" left formation and headed off for Bizerte to attack the seaplane base. About 20 fighters approached from the west, so he turned, sighted a Ju 88 and attacked, destroying it.' Johnson was promoted to flight lieutenant the next day.

On 20 November No 227 Sqn was out in force again. The first element encountered two Caproni Ca.314s, and both were shot down. A second section led by Johnson found a small merchant vessel near Pantelleria, which was attacked and left listing and ablaze. The 785-ton *Lago Tana*, which was carrying troops to Lampedusa, was sunk with heavy loss of life by another strike later in the afternoon.

With Axis forces now in full retreat in North Africa following defeat at the Battle of El Alamein, the Libyan port of Benghazi was occupied on the 21st, and the next day four of No 227 Sqn's Beaufighters, led by Carl Johnson, flew a sweep towards Tunisia. Piloting his regular EL232/J, he engaged two Ju 52/3ms and shot both of them down in less than a minute. Johnson had become an ace. The unit's record book noted 'Two Ju 52s destroyed by "J" (Flt Lt C L Johnson and Plt Off L H Hunt), both bursting into flames, the two aircraft being in the air at the same time.'

However, Johnson's glory was to be brief. During an escort mission flown the very next day in bad weather, Johnson and his navigator, Sgt Ralph Webb, emerged from the murk to spot a merchant ship escorted by an E-boat. The American immediately attacked the escort, his shells raking the warship and inflicting heavy damage. Despite this, the crew of the E-boat managed to fire off a number of rounds at the Beaufighter, which was hit and crashed into the sea. Both (*text continues on page 49*)

Night camouflaged Beaufighter IFs of No 89 Sqn are pictured here dispersed on a North African airfield in early 1943. One of the unit's successful pilots during this period was Sgt Paul Park, an American serving with the RCAF. He shot down three enemy bombers (*B J Wild*)

1
Beaufighter IIF
T3145/KP-K of
Wg Cdr P Y
Davoud, No 409
Sqn RCAF,
Coleby Grange,
March 1942

3
Mosquito II
DD712/YP-R of
Plt Off S J
Cornforth, No 23
Sqn, Bradwell
Bay, 15/16
October 1942

2
Havoc I
BT462/YP-Z of
Sgt G R Wright
RCAF, No 23
Sqn, Ford, 21/22
June 1942

4
Beaufighter VIC
EL232/J of Flt Lt C L
Johnson, No 227 Sqn,
Luqa, Malta,
November 1942

EL232

5
Mosquito II DZ234/
YP-Y of Plt Off S J
Cornforth, No 23 Sqn,
Luqa, Malta, March
1943

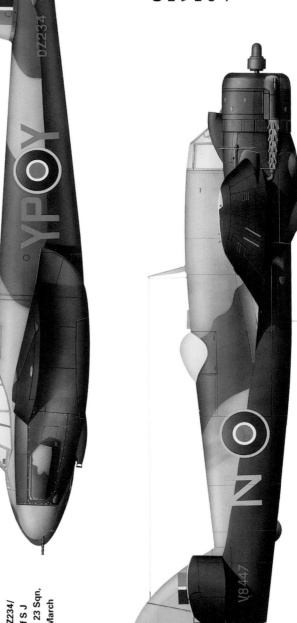

DZ234

YP·Y

6
Beaufighter VIF
V8447/N of Plt Off P T
Park RCAF, No 89 Sqn,
Castel Benito, Libya,
June/July 1943

V8447

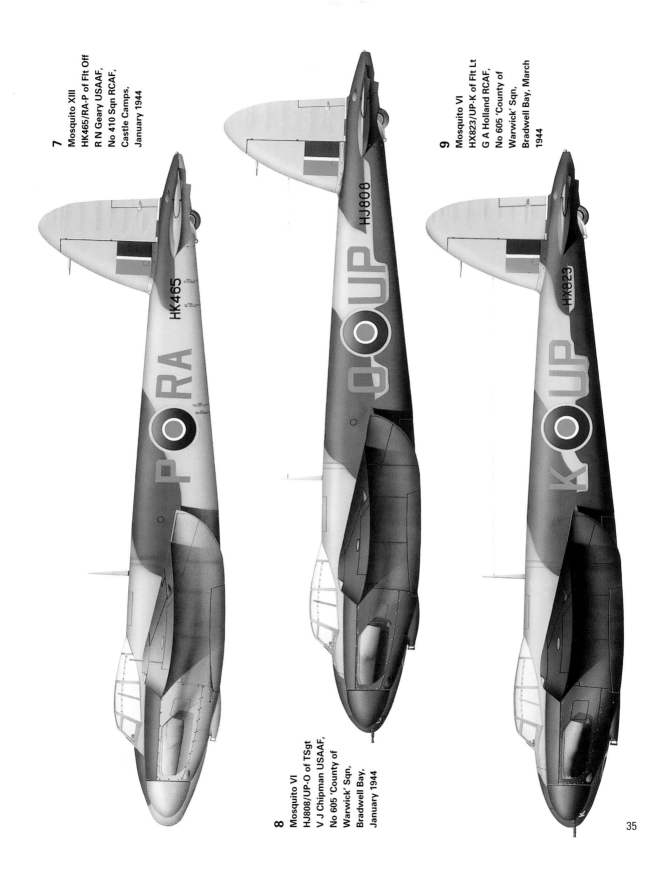

7
Mosquito XIII
HK465/RA-P of Flt Off
R N Geary USAAF,
No 410 Sqn RCAF,
Castle Camps,
January 1944

8
Mosquito VI
HJ808/UP-O of TSgt
V J Chipman USAAF,
No 605 'County of
Warwick' Sqn,
Bradwell Bay,
January 1944

9
Mosquito VI
HX823/UP-K of Flt Lt
G A Holland RCAF,
No 605 'County of
Warwick' Sqn,
Bradwell Bay, March
1944

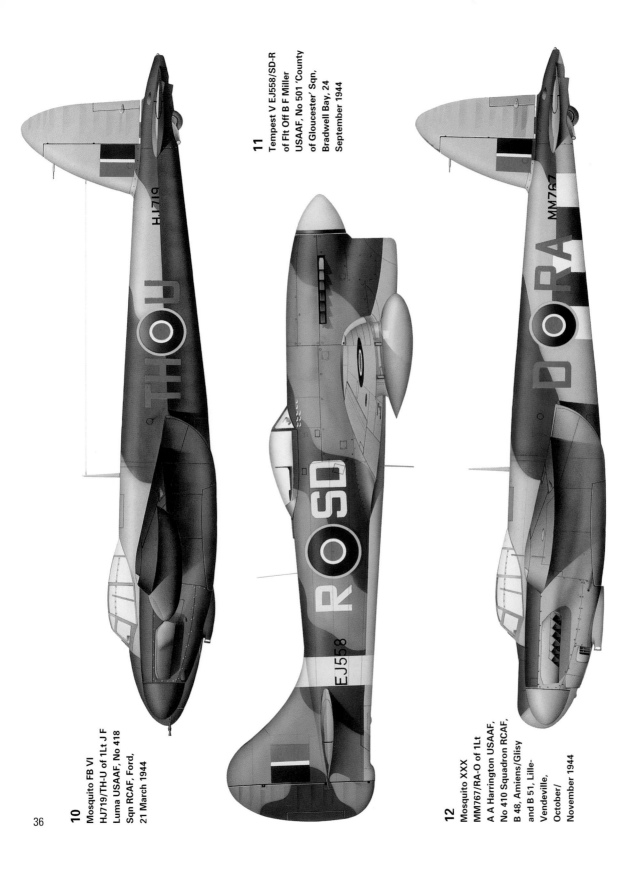

10
Mosquito FB VI
HJ719/TH-U of 1Lt J F
Luma USAAF, No 418
Sqn RCAF, Ford,
21 March 1944

11
Tempest V EJ558/SD-R
of Flt Off B F Miller
USAAF, No 501 'County
of Gloucester' Sqn,
Bradwell Bay, 24
September 1944

12
Mosquito XXX
MM767/RA-O of 1Lt
A A Harrington USAAF,
No 410 Squadron RCAF,
B 48, Amiens/Glisy
and B 51, Lille-
Vendeville,
October/
November 1944

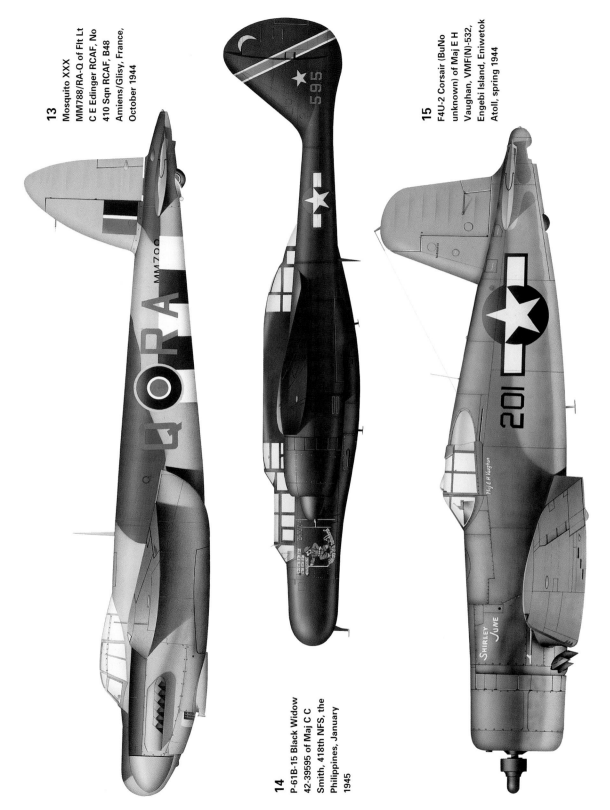

13
Mosquito XXX
MM788/RA-Q of Flt Lt
C E Edinger RCAF, No
410 Sqn RCAF, B48
Amiens/Glisy, France,
October 1944

14
P-61B-15 Black Widow
42-39595 of Maj C C
Smith, 418th NFS, the
Philippines, January
1945

15
F4U-2 Corsair (BuNo
unknown) of Maj E H
Vaughan, VMF(N)-532,
Engebi Island, Eniwetok
Atoll, spring 1944

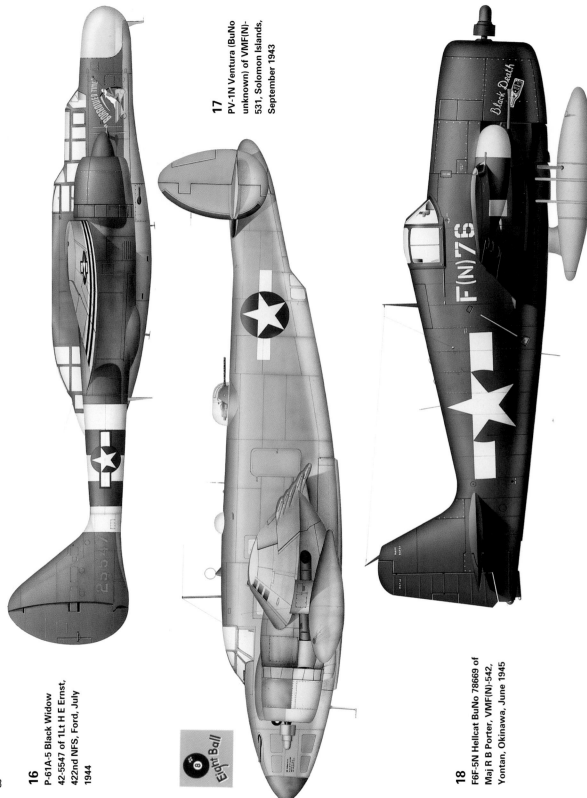

16
**P-61A-5 Black Widow
42-5547 of 1Lt H E Ernst,
422nd NFS, Ford, July
1944**

17
**PV-1N Ventura (BuNo
unknown) of VMF(N)-
531, Solomon Islands,
September 1943**

18
**F6F-5N Hellcat BuNo 78669 of
Maj R B Porter, VMF(N)-542,
Yontan, Okinawa, June 1945**

19
P-61A-10 Black Widow 42-5565 of 2Lt R G Bolinder, 422nd NFS, Etain, France, late 1944

20
P-61B-6 Black Widow 42-39408 of Capt S Solomon, 548th NFS, Ie Shima, Okinawa, spring 1945

21
F6F-5N Hellcat BuNo 78704 of Capt R Baird, VMF(N)-533, Ie Shima, Okinawa, July 1945

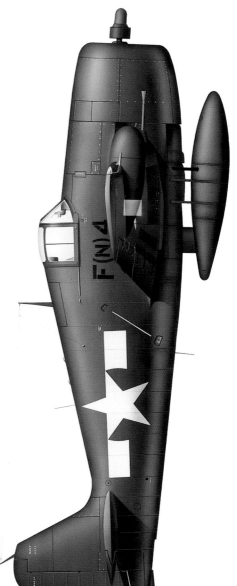

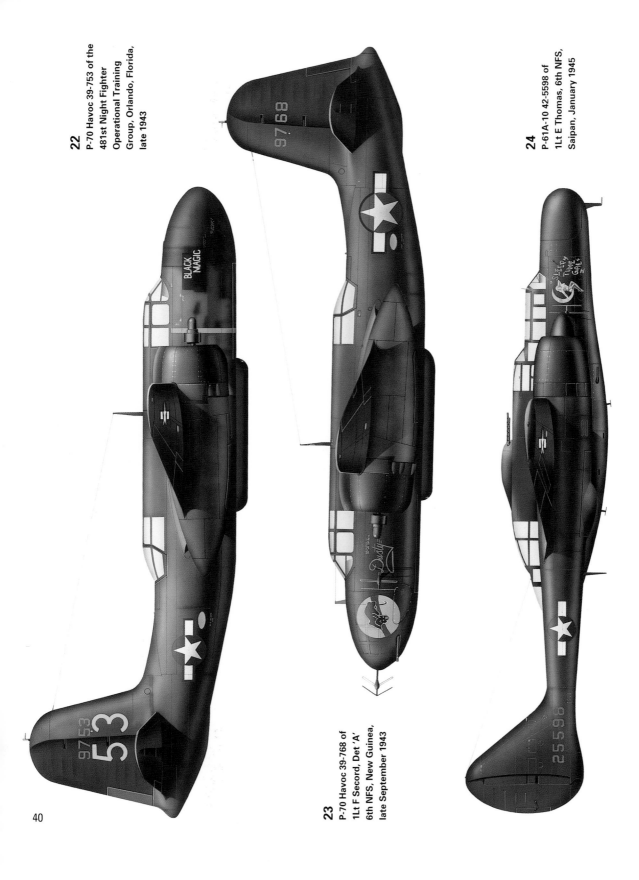

22
P-70 Havoc 39-753 of the
481st Night Fighter
Operational Training
Group, Orlando, Florida,
late 1943

23
P-70 Havoc 39-768 of
1Lt F Secord, Det 'A'
6th NFS, New Guinea,
late September 1943

24
P-61A-10 42-5598 of
1Lt E Thomas, 6th NFS,
Saipan, January 1945

25

Beaufighter VIF V8828
of the 417th NFS,
Corsica, early 1944

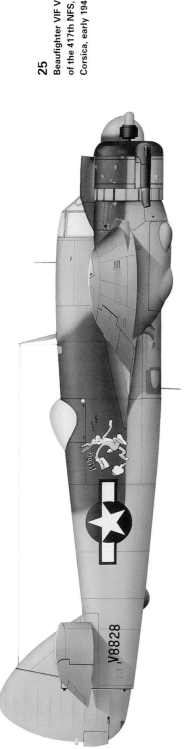

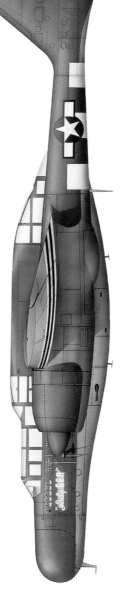

26

P-61A-5 Black Widow
42-5544 of Lt P A Smith,
422nd NFS, A 78
Florennes, Belgium, late
December 1945

27

F6F-5N Hellcat BuNo
70147 of Lt W E Henry,
VF(N)-41, USS
Independence (CVL-22),
Philippine Sea,
September 1944

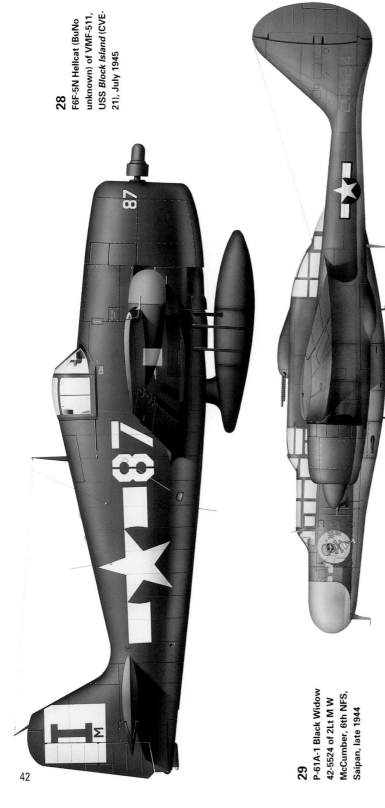

28
F6F-5N Hellcat (BuNo unknown) of VMF-511, USS *Block Island* (CVE-21), July 1945

30
F6F-3N Hellcat BuNo 42158 of Lt R L Reiserer, VF(N)-76 Det 2, USS *Hornet* (CV-12), western Pacific, July 1944

29
P-61A-1 Black Widow 42-5524 of 2Lt M W McCumber, 6th NFS, Saipan, late 1944

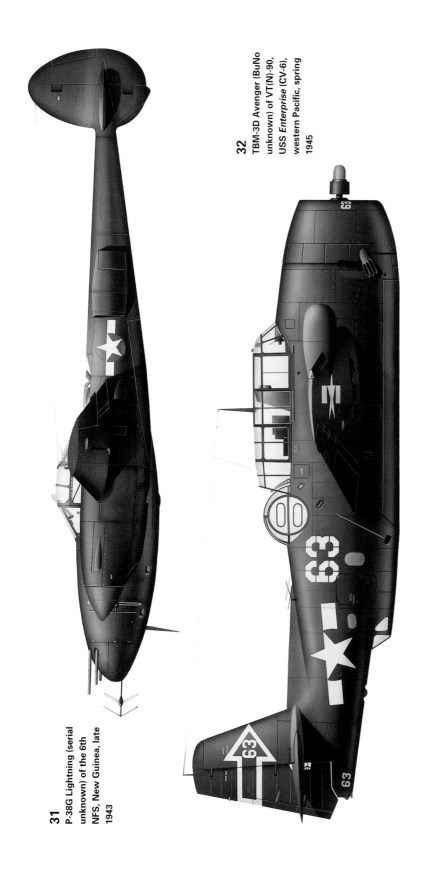

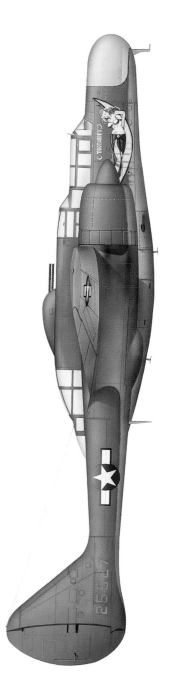

31
P-38G Lightning (serial unknown) of the 6th NFS, New Guinea, late 1943

32
TBM-3D Avenger (BuNo unknown) of VT(N)-90, USS *Enterprise* (CV-6), western Pacific, spring 1945

33
P-61A-1 Black Widow 44-5527 of 2Lt D Haberman, 6th NFS, Saipan, late 1944

43

1

2

3

4

5

6

7

8

9

10

11

12

Johnson and Webb were killed. The record book recorded this tragic event in only the briefest terms;

'Five aircraft airborne on offensive sweep. Convoy was sighted but not attacked. Aircraft "F2" (FLt Lt C L Johnson and Sgt Webb) was hit by intense AAA fire and spun into the sea from 900 ft (280 m).'

By this time Allied troops had landed in French North Africa and were advancing from the west to increase pressure on the Axis forces. On 26 November a detachment of Beaufighters from No 89 Sqn arrived in Algiers to provide night defence. It started flying patrols the following night, and enjoyed immediate success. Among the five enemy bombers shot down on 27/28 November were two (an He 111 and a Ju 88) that fell to the guns of Sgt Paul Park, a 22-year-old American serving with the RCAF, and his navigator, Sgt Rumbold.

The squadron gained further successes during December, and on the 5th a detachment moved east to cover the port of Bone. Another flight was sent to Benina, in Libya, and several successes were achieved early in 1943. One of these was credited to Paul Park, who shot down an He 111 off Tripoli on the night of 8 February in V8376/Z. This proved to be his third, and final, success.

Park had been scrambled at 0200 hrs to the north of Tripoli in bright starlight with a new moon. He climbed to 10,000 ft (3000 m) when Rumbold gained a head-on contact. Park then spotted the intruder. As it flew close by, he turned hard to port, but the evading bomber did likewise and contact with it was lost.

The American pilot later described how they had 'regained contact at 8500 ft (2600 m), crossing slowly from starboard to port on a course of 270 degrees, and the bandit was about 400 ft (120 m) below us. We closed in rapidly, keeping below and slightly to port of the bandit in order to keep the bandit between us and the moon. Evidently, the bandit saw us

No 23 Sqn, equipped with Mosquito IIs like DZ228/YP-D, flew effective night intruder missions over Sicily from Malta in the early months of 1943. One of its successful pilots was Flg Off Stanley Cornforth, who was lost in action over Sicily in the spring (*via John Hamlin*)

at about 500 ft (150 m) range and started to turn hard to starboard. We followed him and closed in to 100 yrd (90 m) and opened fire. Its starboard motor burst into flame. The bandit spiralled to starboard with its engine burning fiercely. At 5000 ft (1500 m) it burst into flames and dove straight down into sea. The bandit crashed into the sea about ten miles (16 km) east-northeast of Tripoli and burned on the water for several minutes.'

Back in Malta, the island's intruder capabilities had increased greatly by the turn of the year with the arrival of the Mosquito IIs of No 23 Sqn. Stanley Cornforth arrived in mid-January 1943 and began flying intruder sorties over Sicilian airfields. On the night of the 31st he left Luqa, but on the way he spotted a pair of Savoia S.82 (identified by the American as Ju 52/3ms) transports heading for North Africa. Cornforth not only shot both of them down in quick succession, but also put the escorting Bf 109 to flight! The squadron's operational record book stated simply that 'Flg Off Cornforth went on the first patrol and, on the way in, met and destroyed two Ju 52s. An Me 109 which was escorting the first did not stay to see the fun.'

Cornforth and his navigator remained active throughout February and into March, and on the 2nd of the latter month, shortly before 1100 hrs, they left Luqa for another intruder mission to Sicily. Arriving over Castel Veltrano, Cornforth spotted an enemy aircraft – possibly a Ju 88 from I./KG 54, which had been raiding Tripoli. He hit it with a burst of fire but could only claim it as damaged. However, on the evening of 1 April the pair left for an intruder sortie to eastern Sicily and did not return. The squadron history noted;

'Although no losses are more acceptable than others, there is a particular poignancy as they include one of the original Bradwell crews – Flg Offs Cornforth and Davies. Luck would always play a significant part.'

In Libya, Paul Park, now commissioned as a pilot officer, was regularly scrambled but saw little of the enemy. Later in the year No 89 Sqn moved to the Far East, but by then Park was tour-expired, so he did not go with the unit.

By the summer of 1943, Luqa-based No 272 Sqn listed among its RCAF pilots Flg Off Ernest Edgett. Thought to have been an American citizen from Springfield, Massachusetts, he flew his first operational sortie on 6 August. His was one of four Beaufighters to attack the seaplane

Beaufighter VIF V8447/N of No 89 Sqn was regularly flown during mid-1943 by Plt Off Paul Park, an American serving with the RCAF. The aircraft is pictured at Castel Benito, Libya, on 3 August 1943 when it crashed on landing after a tyre had burst. Its pilot on this occasion was 17-victory ace Wg Cdr Dennis David, who had assumed command of the unit 15 days earlier (via M Hodgson)

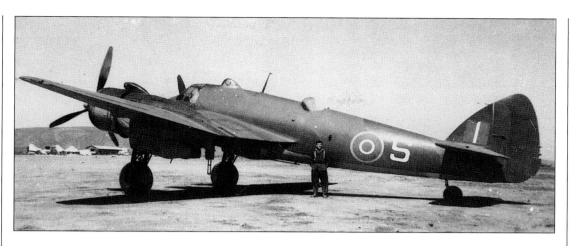

RCAF pilot Flg Off Ernest Edgett, who is thought to have originated from Massachusetts, flew from Malta with No 272 Sqn. He achieved several victories with the unit flying Beaufighter VIs such as X8105/S, which is pictured at Luqa in 1943 (*author's collection*)

base at Corfu. They bombed hangars and strafed moored seaplanes, with the crews involved claiming to have damaged one Do 18, left another one sinking and a third burning vigorously on the water.

By early September No 272 Sqn was based in eastern Sicily, and from there, on the 24th, it flew what the unit's operational record book described as the finest day in its history. Among those who filed claims for the action over the Tyrrhenian Sea was Flg Off Ernest Edgett. The record book stated;

'The Beaus met a formation of eight Ju 52s, with a single-engined fighter above and ahead. Flg Off Edgett attacked a Ju 52 flying on the port side (rear) of the formation. After two bursts from 300 yrd (280m), the enemy aircraft was seen to burst into flames and crash into the sea. Our machine then turned off, having been hit in the starboard wing by return fire from one of the enemy formation. However, Flg Off Edgett returned to the fray and attacked another Ju 52 to starboard of the formation and sent it down in flames into the sea, afterwards damaging yet another, which disappeared over a hill on the coast pouring smoke.'

Overall, No 272 Sqn claimed nine Junkers transports destroyed, one probable and one damaged.

That same month the nightfighter Beaufighters of No 46 Sqn were supporting operations in the Dodecanese, flying night intruder sorties over Rhodes. For this task a detachment was based in Cyprus, although its effectiveness was somewhat limited due to the extreme range to the target areas. It was over Rhodes that Plt Off J S 'Tex' Holland from Florida made his combat debut with an attack on Maritza airfield. On 3 October the squadron received a mauling during an attack on German invasion shipping off the island of Cos. Operations continued, however, and off Leros on the 10th 'Tex' Holland shared in the destruction of a Ju 87 dive-bomber and damaged another.

Although this was his first success, Holland was a highly-experienced pilot. He had originally flown Wellingtons with No 70 Sqn in the Middle East, and was one of the few American pilots to receive the DFM. Six days later the unit records stated 'Flg Off Holland, on offensive sweep, damaged a Ju 88 which was engaged in shooting up Flt Sgt Jackson'.

However, on the 18th Holland met some enemy fighters and, as the record book again noted;

'They attacked two Me 109s which turned and attacked. Flg Off Holland's aircraft was hit and his observer, Flt Sgt Bruck, was mortally wounded. The aircraft was successfully ditched and the crew took to the dinghy. Flt Sgt Bruck died shortly afterwards of his wounds and Flg Off Holland was picked up safely by an ASR launch from Castelrosso.'

In spite of his ordeal, Holland soon resumed operations, and in early December was posted to No 227 Sqn in Libya. On Christmas Eve he was part of a four-aircraft offensive sweep off eastern Greece that attacked a caique in the Kithira Channel.

Further west, Ernest Edgett remained with No 272 Sqn, and was clearly highly-regarded, as the record book's final entry for the year sadly recorded, 'whilst flying off Catania his Beaufighter ditched. Flg Off Edgett's loss came as a great shock to the entire squadron. He was a very capable pilot, and showed promise going a long way.'

'Tex' Holland remained active with No 227 Sqn, and he experienced an air combat off Crete on 4 March 1944 which the record described as follows;

'Flt Lt J S Holland took off at 2245 hrs on night intruding operations. Later, a Ju 52 was sighted heading for Maleme. Our aircraft hit the enemy aircraft with a short burst of cannon fire, causing it to crash into the sea, where it burned for one minute and then exploded.'

This was the last kill by an American night/strike fighter pilot with the RAF in the Mediterranean. Holland remained with the unit until it was later disbanded, after which he returned to Canada as an instructor.

USAAF OPERATIONS

British and Commonwealth nightfighter squadrons were not the only Allied units operating in the Mediterranean theatre to be equipped with British-built aircraft. US units also flew Beaufighters and Mosquitoes,

Plt Off 'Tex' Holland flew Beaufighter IF nightfighters like V8502/H whilst serving with No 46 Sqn. He achieved several victories over the Greek islands before returning to Canada as an instructor (*ww2images.com*)

The 416th NFS flew nightfighter operations in the Mediterranean theatre. During the course of the war, the unit was equipped with the P-70, Beaufighter, Mosquito and A-36. This photograph was taken at Pontedera, in Italy, when it was operating Mosquito XXXs (*Earl Elliott*)

which, until the arrival of the P-61 Black Widow, were the only Allied types to be effective against the Luftwaffe.

In early 1943, when the 414th, 415th, 416th and 417th NFSs were activated, their crews were trained on US-built P-70s, but flew combat missions in British aircraft. Although no aces emerged from these units, their activities in the Mediterranean theatre would still be regarded as extremely valuable. The top-scoring unit was the 414th, which was credited with 13 night kills. This total was greater than those of the other US nightfighter squadrons in the theatre (which, together, accumulated 25) because the 414th had converted to the P-61 in time to participate in the Battle of the Bulge in the ETO in late 1944 and early 1945. During this period it scored five kills.

The other squadrons were not to receive their Black Widows until the latter stages of the war when the Luftwaffe's strength was nearing exhaustion. Their achievements while equipped with Beaufighters were regarded as outstanding – 32 kills and 10 probables. They flew from bases in North Africa and Italy as the war progressed and, apart from the 414th NFS, they did not start conversion onto the P-61 until the spring of 1945, by which time most German aircraft were grounded for lack of fuel.

The Beaufighter enjoyed a long production run, during which more than 5500 aircraft were built between 1940 and 1946. The aircraft had a range of more than 1700 miles (2720 km) and a top speed of 320 mph (515 km/h). Heavily armed with four 20 mm cannon, it was also capable of carrying rockets or bombs, thus allowing the aircraft to be used effectively during both daylight and night operations. American pilots were pleased to fly the Beaufighter in combat, and its two Bristol Hercules

Four American nightfighter squadrons flew Beaufighters in the Mediterranean theatre. This example, serving with the 417th NFS, was photographed while the unit was operating from Corsica (*Richard Ziebart*)

radial engines were found to be dependable power units. This was a particularly desirable attribute in the Mediterranean theatre, where long flights over the sea were the norm.

Despite the dearth of USAAF aces in this theatre, several pilots were credited with two or three kills. There were few opportunities for accumulating bigger scores, and most of the kills were achieved when the units were operating off the south coast of France. The Germans launched numerous nocturnal air attacks on Allied shipping and North African bases from airfields in France and Italy.

One of the most successful American Beaufighter pilots was 2Lt Rayford W Jeffrey of the 417th NFS, who was credited with two confirmed kills against night-flying Ju 88s. During the late afternoon of 28 March 1944, Jeffrey was on convoy patrol guarding a large number of ships ferrying supplies and equipment. Apart from its outcome, his mission that day was fairly typical of those flown by the four squadrons. He explained;

'I was on convoy escort patrol between North Africa and the southern coast of Spain. The Ju 88 that I eventually shot down was acting as a pathfinder for a force of German bombers attempting to attack a large Allied convoy. Ground control passed me a vector to intercept a single bogey that was on course for our ships.

'About 20 miles (32 km) northeast of the convoy, my radar observer, 2Lt Bill Henderson, got a radar contact. Minutes later, after closing fast, I got visual confirmation that it was a Ju 88. The enemy was using this type of aircraft as a pathfinder for the main force. The hostile contact was coming head-on at an altitude of 50 ft (15 m) or less! I made a turn to try to come in behind him. The Ju 88 pilot saw me and started a 180-degree turn. That was to my advantage because I could easily slide in behind him.

'I closed to within 700 ft (215 m) and opened fire. I felt the drop in airspeed resulting from the recoil of my 20 mm cannon, which were loaded alternately with armour piercing, incendiary and high explosive rounds. Most of them missed, but a few did hit the target. I noticed an object being thrown from the Ju 88. I moved even closer, to within 400 ft (120 m), and heard the staccato "plunk, plunk, plunk" of gunfire from the bogey's top turret hitting my Beaufighter. Suddenly, I felt a searing pain as a round struck my foot. At that time I fired a long burst at him, exhausting all of my 20 mm ammunition. I was rewarded with the sight of large parts coming off the target's wings and fuselage. Among them was the canopy from the rear gunner's turret that had been hitting me.'

The Ju 88 pilot could no longer maintain altitude, and his aircraft crashed into the sea and sank immediately. Jeffrey quickly climbed to 3000 ft (900 m) and reported his success to GCI. Ten minutes after resuming his patrol, GCI informed Jeffrey about further bogeys heading in his general direction – the enemy was obviously determined to locate the Allied convoy. Soon there were too many blips on the radar scope to count. All the Beaufighters in the area responded, but dusk was fast approaching.

By the time night fell the enemy force had withdrawn without finding any Allied ships to attack. The Ju 88 represented 2Lt Rayford W Jeffrey's second confirmed kill in the Beaufighter. If he had not run out of ammunition there might have been more by the end of the mission.

ENTER THE BLACK WIDOW

The USA had entered the war with its fighter technology and tactics lagging behind those of the other combatants. Nowhere was this more apparent than in the arena of nocturnal operations. The US Army had already made some attempts to catch up. In August 1940, Maj Gen Delos C Emmons, CO of the US Army Air Corps General Headquarters at Langley Field, Virginia, had headed a three-man military mission sent to the UK to evaluate at first hand the type of equipment Britain needed to continue the war against Germany. During its stay, the mission was able to see for itself the terrible damage wrought by the Luftwaffe's night *Blitz* on London, and Emmons was briefed on the development of AI radar.

Once the mission had returned home, the Massachusetts Institute of Technology (MIT) was given the task of developing a US version of Britain's AI radar. The end result of MIT's work was the efficient, but bulky, Radiation Laboratory SCR-720 radar, whose sheer size dictated the development of a specialist nightfighter to carry it. On 2 October 1940, an outline specification was issued by the USAAC for an aircraft large enough for both the radar and its operator. It was a challenging brief, for the aircraft had to have considerable range, high speed and a rapid rate of climb, plus a heavy armament.

Just 34 days later John K Northrop, who had founded his own company the previous year, was able to present a proposal. Although his firm was relatively new, such was Northrop's reputation within the industry that on 11 January 1941 a contract was placed for two prototypes to be designated XP-61. These aircraft were overtaken by events in the Pacific in December of that year, however. Now, the need for nightfighters was so pressing that by the time Northrop's prototype flew for the first time on 21 May 1942, an order for 670 aircraft had already been placed.

While the USAAF was awaiting the delivery of Northrop's purpose-built nightfighter, it began to form squadrons in preparation for the P-61's arrival in the frontline. Among the first pilots trained to fly nightfighters in the USA was Capt James E Alford, who was assigned to

The secret of the Black Widow's success was its state-of-the-art Radiation Laboratory SCR-720 radar. This equipment, however, required constant maintenance in the field, and the hot, humid conditions of the Pacific took their toll. This photograph was taken in Hawaii just after the 6th NFS had received its first P-61s in May 1944. They would soon depart for forward operating bases (*Vance Austin*)

the 6th NFS upon its redesignation in January 1943. He explained some of the background to the USAAF's fledgling programme;

'The early formative months were divided into several phases. The first was initiated right after the Japanese attack on Pearl Harbor. The American high command felt that there was a strong possibility the Japanese would follow up the attack with an invasion of the Hawaiian Islands, or at least conduct some long range night reconnaissance missions. Opposing this threat was a small

composite squadron of ancient P-26s, P-36 Hawks and a handful of new P-40Bs. This was both inefficient and undesirable. Only the P-40s would have had a chance of intercepting the faster Japanese aircraft.

'Thus, the second phase was initiated when Seventh Fighter Command determined that a solid programme had to be developed immediately. The first combat squadron to be designated a true nightfighter squadron was the 6th, which had been headquartered in Hawaii since 1917.'

The USAAF's first attempt at developing a useable nightfighter was the P-70, which was basically a Douglas A-20 Havoc fitted with radar and 20 mm cannon. It was a rush job, and strictly a stop-gap measure pending the arrival of the P-61. At this stage of the war, the greatest need for nightfighters was being felt in the Pacific, but senior officers in the USAAF found it difficult to persuade the Army to relinquish valuable A-20 light attack bombers which had already been highly successful in North Africa.

Nevertheless, 59 were earmarked for conversion into P-70s. Another 40 were ordered soon afterwards, and these were to have six 0.50-cal nose-mounted machine guns in addition to the cannon located in a gun tub fitted over the now-redundant bomb-bay – these aircraft were designated P-70As. The cannon was subsequently deleted from the P-70B to lighten the aircraft and improve its chances of making successful interceptions at higher altitudes. The aircraft saw service on Guadalcanal and in New Guinea, but when P-61s started rolling off the assembly lines in early 1944, the P-70s were relegated to training in the US. Indeed, it is estimated that up to 90 per cent of US nightfighter crews cut their teeth on the type.

With the Black Widow delayed by structural and radar problems, something more effective than the P-70 was desperately needed to counter Japanese intruders. In late 1943 the USAAF began experimenting with P-38 Lightnings operating in conjunction with ground-based searchlights. The single-seat fighters lacked airborne radar, so their chances of success were limited. However, at this stage of the war only the P-38s had any realistic chance of catching the fast, high-flying Mitsubishi G4M Navy Type 1 'Betty' bombers.

Maj Carroll Smith, CO of the 418th NFS and the sole USAAF nightfighter ace of the Pacific, recalled the early operations in this theatre;

As a stopgap measure pending delivery of the P-61, a number of A-20 Havocs were converted into nightfighters through the fitment of radar early in the war. Redesignated P-70s, most of these aircraft were assigned to units in the Pacific, such as Detachment A of the 6th NFS, which flew this particular example from bases in New Guinea during the early summer of 1943. Detachment B also had P-70s, and it was sent to defend Guadalcanal from nocturnal raiders in February 1943 (*Fred Secord*)

'By early January 1944 we were operational at Dobodura, in New Guinea, with both the P-70 and the P-38. We flew local night patrols and then used our P-38s to hunt for targets out of an advanced base at Finschafen – a typical mission was to depart from Dobodura in the afternoon and then stage out of Finschafen. We relieved day fighters working hot spots during the late afternoon so that they could return to their bases before dark.

'We would patrol in two-ships with P-38s all night until relieved at dawn by the day fighters. You had to be careful because the defenders of the Jap airfields proved to be tricky foes. One night I got lucky and shot down a "Val" (Allied code name for the Aichi D3Y Navy Type 99 dive-bomber) over Alexishafen. The next night we were back in the same area when we spotted three "Sallys" (Mitsubishi Ki-21 Army Type 97 heavy bombers) parked on the edge of the strip. I lined up to make a strafing pass and then realised we'd been suckered in through a hail of anti-aircraft fire. The bombers were hulks that were probably being used for spare parts. Fortunately, I was hugging the ground, and the Jap gunners were shooting at each other as I was slightly ahead of their aim.'

The 418th NFS's mixed force of P-70s, P-38s and B-25s in 1943-44 made it unique, and the unit only standardised on one type once P-61s started arriving in the Pacific in early 1944. Ultimately, the big Northrop fighter was the aircraft that would be flown by the highest-scoring USAAF nightfighter ace of any theatre of war.

Earlier experimentation with P-38s operating in conjunction with searchlights might have produced limited success, but it did achieve its intended goal of telling the Japanese that the USAAF possessed a nightfighter that was at least capable of matching the altitude and speed of the 'Betty'. But as most of the 418th NFS pilots had no P-38 experience, the unit was obliged to borrow pilots from other squadrons. One such individual was 1Lt Vernon Jenner, who was a member of the high-scoring 80th FS/8th FG, which was based nearby. Jenner was to be involved in one of the few success stories from the squadron's brief P-38 period when, on the night of 24 November

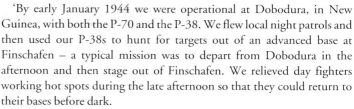

A pair of P-61Bs fly over the water during a training sortie in late 1944. Note that both aircraft are fitted with 0.50-cal top turrets, which were produced later in the war. This shot was taken by a Northrop photographer off California (*Northrop Corporation*)

1943, he was at altitude when enemy bombers arrived. They were illuminated by the searchlight beams and Jenner was able to shoot down two of them within minutes.

Two nights later, Maj Carroll Smith again caught one of the attackers framed in the searchlight beams, and he was credited with a probable. On 28 November, again working with the searchlights, he scored two kills. As a result of this success, the unit's achievements earned it praise from Thirteenth Air Force Headquarters. Of the five Japanese aircraft caught in the searchlight beams between 24 and 28 November, four had been destroyed and the fifth logged as a probable. Considering that USAAF nightfighter techniques were still at a crude and experimental stage in late 1943, the 418th NFS's achievements were little short of amazing.

IN THE ETO

The 422nd and 425th NFSs were sent to England in the early spring of 1944 to support the impending Allied invasion of France, and they re-equipped with the Black Widow in mid-1944. The 422nd NFS received its first examples on 23 May, while sister unit the 425th welcomed P-61s on 15 June.

Although the 422nd had received the new nightfighter two weeks before the Normandy landings, the unit was far from ready for combat with its new equipment by the time troops stormed the beaches. As a result, the RAF continued to bear the brunt of the nightfighter effort over France immediately after D-Day. Indeed, it was not until 16 July that the 422nd scored its first P-61 kill, with the 425th following suit on 5 August. These victories were scored over pilotless V1 flying bombs intercepted before they reached the English south coast, rather than manned aircraft. During this period, with the P-61 crews still in training, the two squadrons accounted for a combined total of nine V1s.

With flying bombs routinely being encountered, training flights often proved to be eventful. 2Lt Herman E Ernst, who was to become one of the 422nd's nightfighter aces with five aerial victories and one V1 kill, recalls one such training mission flown over the channel while his unit was still accumulating experience with its new equipment;

1Lt Herman Ernst scored all five of his night kills (and a V1) while flying in his assigned 422nd NFS P-61A-5 42-5547 *"BORROWED TIME"*. This photograph was taken at Colerne in late June 1944, just after the D-Day landings. Note the trio of Mosquito NF XIIIs from No 604 Sqn parked behind the Black Widow (*John Anderson*)

By shooting down a V1 flying bomb, 1Lt Herman Ernst (left) and his radar observer 1Lt Edward Kopsel of the 422nd NFS scored the P-61's first aerial kill in Europe. They went on to score five victories over manned German aircraft to achieve ace status (*John Anderson*)

'Our squadron's first operations involved chasing buzz bombs off the coast. At the time we were flying out of Ford aerodrome on the south coast near Brighton. I spotted a V1 approaching from France and gave chase. My air speed was very high as I closed on it. Suddenly, there was a loud bang and my aircraft became hard to handle. I thought I was being shot down on my very first mission! I aborted the interception and returned to base. After safely landing and pulling into our parking slot, I found that the tail cone, right behind my radar observer, had disintegrated. This had caused the buffeting and loud wind noise.

'We replaced it with a flat piece of Plexiglas, and that worked until we received new tail cones from Northrop. The next night we were up again, hoping to catch a V1, and the mission went much better than the previous one. We spotted one of the buzz bombs coming in below us. I turned sharply and went into a steep dive. That closed the gap quickly. When the range closed to within 20 mm cannon range, I fired a long burst and the V1 exploded in a huge fireball. I believe that this was the first aerial kill scored by the P-61 in the European Theatre.'

Once operational, the two Black Widow squadrons were soon sent to France, with the 422nd NFS moving to A 15 Maupertus on 25 July and the 425th NFS to Vanne on 18 August.

Although now closer to the fighting on the ground, P-61 crews did not see much action in the air, for during the September-October period, the Luftwaffe concentrated its nocturnal activities on countering RAF heavy bombers attacking German cities. As a result, pilots like Herman Ernst would not score again until November, by which point the 422nd was flying from A 78 Florennes, in Belgium, and the 425th had been sent to Coulommiers, in France.

Ernst's victim on 27 November was a Bf 110. He and his crew were flying a 'barrier patrol' between the frontlines and the Rhine, hoping to intercept Luftwaffe night intruders intent on attacking Allied road traffic. By this time the Germans were well aware of the Black Widow's presence, and its capability, but they were willing to risk encountering in an attempt to stem the Allied advance. Ernst recalled;

'We were patrolling at about 10,000 ft (3000 m) when GCI came on the radio and told us a bogey was approaching at 4000 ft (1200m) from a distance of 20 miles (32 km). I immediately dropped the nose and went down to 3500 ft (1075 m), and by that time the distance between us and the intruder was only 2.5 miles (4 km). My radar observer, 2Lt Ed Kopsel, already had a lock on the bogey as it passed overhead.

'We got on his tail and narrowed the gap down to 1400 ft (430 m). I eased back on the throttles to slow the closure rate, and when the gap hit 800 ft (250 m) we were able to get a positive visual – it was a Bf 110

1Lt Herman Ernst and his crew chief pose beside their P-61 at the 422nd's new base at Chateaudun, in France, in the late summer of 1944. Ernst would not achieve his first victory over a manned German aircraft until late November. His V1 kill (along with his mission tally) is clearly displayed on the nose of his aircraft, however (*Herman Ernst*)

nightfighter. He was flying at 200 mph (320 km/h) on a course of 200 degrees at an altitude of 3700 ft (1140 m). He was evidently looking for movement on the roads, and had no idea I was onto him.

'With the bogey square in my sights, I gave him a two-second burst with my 20 mm cannon. I observed strikes on the fuselage and wing roots. Continuing to close down to less than 600 ft (185 m), I fired another quick burst, which converged on his port engine and wing root. Before I could blink an eye, a huge explosion consumed the Bf 110 in a fireball, and he went straight down through the broken undercast. Now, this brought a dangerous situation for us because the cloud layer was about 3000 ft (900 m) above the ground, so I couldn't take the chance of following him down to confirm the kill. However, we did get a confirmation from ground troops in the area. It was a clean kill!'

If a V1 could have been counted as a manned aircraft, this crew would have achieved ace status. They are radar observer 2Lt Leonard Mapes (left) and pilot 1Lt Robert Elmore, who used P-61A-5 42-5534 *"SHOO-SHOO BABY"* to score four confirmed kills, plus the V1, while serving with the 422nd NFS (*Robert Graham*)

With a bit more luck, at least two more 422nd NFS pilots would have become aces in the final months of the war in Europe. Indeed, the unit was to chalk up the highest score of any US nightfighter squadron. One of these pilots was 1Lt Robert O Elmore, who, with his radar observer 2Lt Leonard F Mapes, flew a Black Widow named *"SHOO-SHOO BABY"*. This crew would be among the first to engage the surge of Luftwaffe aircraft generated by the start of the Battle of the Bulge on 16 December. They already had a V1 to their credit, and now they

were looking for their first manned kill. They were to reach that milestone on the offensive's opening night, as Elmore recalled;

'We were patrolling over the First Army frontline area at about 0100 hrs. It was a pitch-black night, with overcast and no star to be seen. We were particularly low at 5000 ft (1500 m), and taking orders from "Marmite", our GCI. I first noticed activity on the ground when brilliant searchlights began to appear horizontal to the ground shining towards the west. "Marmite" began reporting numerous targets in our area.

'Suddenly, an aircraft passed close overhead, going in the opposite direction. Ground control vectored us towards the unidentified contact and 2Lt Mapes got a lock on it. He guided me in close enough to get a positive ID – it was a Ju 88. I eased back on the throttles to get into a better firing position exactly on the bogey's "six o'clock". I gave it a short burst of 20 mm, which impacted all over the intruder. The hits must have been fatal because the aircraft went into a diving turn. Seconds later we observed two parachutes. It was a fast, clean kill. We didn't get a chance to hang around because we were at the end of our operating limits and had to return to base. Later, we found out that we were one of the first nightfighter crews to witness the start of the Battle of the Bulge."

BATTLE OF THE BULGE

Once the armada of Allied fighter and medium bomber aircraft formerly based in the UK began operating from airfields on mainland Europe, it seemed that the end of the war – and of Hitler's Third Reich – was in sight. Day fighters escorted the bombers, and then attacked any suitable ground targets their pilots could find along the way. With the sky full of Allied aircraft, the weakened Luftwaffe was forced to concentrate its efforts on keeping ground forces supplied to the hours of darkness. Under these circumstances, the German counter-offensive that came to be known as the Battle of the Bulge was as an unpleasant shock to the Allies.

To the US military it was officially known as the Battle of the Ardennes, but whatever it was called, there was no disguising the fact that it was the bloodiest action fought by the US Army in World War 2. More than 19,000 Allied soldiers died in the battle, which raged from 16 December through to 25 January, and the great majority of them were Americans. To the USAAF's 422nd NFS, however, this was a time of great success, which catapulted it to the top of the nightfighter organisation's scoreboard. The squadron's aircrew would complete their combat tour with 43 confirmed kills, plus five V1s.

Part of the reason for this success was that the unit was in the right place at the right time, such as on the night of 17 December when Black Widow ace 2Lt Herman Ernst took off from A 78 Florennes. His mission was to patrol an area between the positions on the frontline occupied by Seventh Corps and the Rhine. Soon after reaching their patrol station, Ernst and his crew were told by GCI of a bogey at 12 miles (19 km) and closing. Ernst explained what happened next;

'I made a fast closure on the incoming intruder and was able to get a visual at one mile. We got onto its tail and closed to less than 600 ft (185 m), where we got a positive identification – it was a Ju 87 Stuka. This guy was up to no good. It was a loaded dive-bomber, and he was out to find our troops and drop his lethal cargo.

'At such close range the Stuka pilot had noticed us, and he began taking violent evasive action. He had been flying at a slow speed – 110 mph (176 km/h) – before we were spotted. He was on a south-southwesterly course at 3000 ft (900 m). He was definitely looking for troop movements on the roads. We were close enough to get off a good burst of 20 mm, which hit him squarely in both wing roots. One of the rounds must have ignited a gas tank, for a plume of flames gushed out of one wing root and this put him into an immediate nose-down spiral. At such a low altitude he went straight into the ground with very little chance of baling out. It was 0523 hrs – the time when it really was darkest just before dawn. We had chalked up another clean kill for the Black Widow.'

Elmore and Mapes of the 422nd were up again on the night of 22/23 December, patrolling between the River Meuse and St Vith-Malmady. Mapes recalled the sequence of events leading up to the pair's second kill;

'After some time on patrol at 10,000 ft (3000 m), our GCI picked up a fast mover coming towards us head-on some 3000 ft (900 m) below our altitude. I got a radar contact at slightly over a mile and completed the head-on interception by directing Elmore to 1000 ft (300 m) astern, where we were able to obtain a visual. We still couldn't get a positive ID because of the bogey's position in relation to the moon. We pulled off to the side and slightly down. At that angle we were able to identify it as an Me 110 flying on a course of 300 degrees at 8000 ft (2500 m). At only 190 mph (300 km/h), it was moving slower than the average bogey.

'We eased back some 100 ft (30 m) dead astern and Elmore gave it a long burst of 20 mm. Before you could blink an eye the Me 110 exploded, and we were flying right through the debris. We had no time to react to the violent impact of our guns. In a few seconds our aircraft suffered category A damage, with our port engine on fire, but Elmore maintained control. Just as we were about to bale out the fire seemed to be burning itself out. A couple of minutes later it was out, but the engine was inoperable. This left us with one engine, and that was far from being 100 per cent. As we swung around to return to base, we received an alarming radio message – every airfield in our home base area was socked in at "zero-zero" by bad weather. The only one available, and it was barely at minimum then, was an RAF base at Brussels.

'We had no choice so we headed that way. We'd never been there before, but we found it through my radar interpretation and help from GCI. When we arrived overhead, our fuel was almost gone and the ceiling was between 100 ft and 200 ft (30 m and 60 m). Needless to say, we had the party to end all parties with the RAF crews that night. The next morning they showed us high-level obstacles that we had flown through – smoke stacks, high buildings, water towers etc. We were certainly lucky to have made it through, as we hadn't seen any of them. Our P-61 was junked – it had had it!

'The durability of the Black Widow and its reliable Pratt & Whitney R-2800 engines, plus the piloting skills of Capt Elmore, had seen us safely through a harrowing situation. We'd achieved another confirmed kill, giving us two thus far, plus the V1.'

As radar observer, Leonard Mapes was positioned in the P-61's rear compartment. Sitting up front, the pilot had a different view of the action. This is how Elmore saw it on the night they claimed the Bf 110;

'We were one of only a few crews able to take-off that night because of deteriorating weather conditions. It was a clear night above 5000 ft (1540 m), with a full moon and excellent visibility. "Marmite" put us onto a target heading southwest at the top of the undercast. We closed on the intruder and 2Lt Mapes got a lock at five miles (8 km). Due to the light from the moon, we were able to determine that it was a Bf 110. I dropped back and came right up his tail from the "six o'clock" position at his altitude, opening fire with my 20 mm. I was too close to fire, but did it anyway."

'The target blew up, and before I could react we were flying through all kinds of flaming debris. Lenny Mapes said we had pieces of Bf 110 hanging across our horizontal stabiliser. My armoured windscreen was cracked pretty bad, and some red hot metal had started a fire in the oil cooling intake – it appeared to be very serious. I told Mapes to be ready to bale out, but the hot metal burned its way through the oil scoop and dropped away, so no panic button! We were way out over the Bastogne area, which put us quite a long distance from our airfield.

'The weather had closed in and the only field open was Brussels, and its ceiling was dropping fast. We were vectored in that direction, and when we arrived the ceiling had dropped to about 150 ft (46 m). We broke through, saw the lights and the controller talked us in with no problems.'

Elmore's was not the only P-61 to encounter bad weather that night. Just minutes before *"SHOO-SHOO BABY"* landed, P-61 ace 1Lt Paul Smith had managed to put *"Lady GEN"* down safely. Having made one pass along the runway, he pulled up, made a sharp 360-degree turn to port and landed – with the ceiling so low, this was a feat of airmanship that required a good deal of piloting skill. The next morning, the crews were able to see in daylight the obstacles they had missed as they groped their way though the darkness.

As Leonard Mapes recalled, *"SHOO-SHOO BABY"* was not to fly again. A week later Luftwaffe aircraft strafed the airfield and inflicted fatal damage on the P-61. Its crew was assigned another aircraft, and they saw more action a few weeks later. By this time Allied forces had cornered a large number of German troops as the offensive collapsed, and Luftwaffe Ju 52/3ms were attempting to airlift the trapped officers to safety under the cover of darkness. This meant the lumbering Junkers tri-motors had to fly very slowly, and at tree-top height.

The US GCI station covering that sector was located on one of the highest hills in the area, which enabled it to track the low-flying transports. Elmore and Mapes found themselves involved in the operation to intercept the Ju 52/3ms, and they destroyed two of them as Elmore recalled;

'We had to close on these aircraft at very slow speeds. On both of our successful interceptions I remember using half-flap, and it was almost like trying to land on a very short airstrip. I know our squadron scored numerous kills during this brief period.'

LADY GEN'S BIG NIGHT

422nd NFS crew 1Lt Paul Smith and 2Lt Robert Tierney had not only joined forces to score a total of five confirmed kills plus a probable, they were also very proficient in air-to-ground operations, as they demonstrated by destroying several locomotives. But on the night of 26/27 December, they were after aerial targets in their P-61 *"Lady GEN"*. With snow on the ground and freezing temperatures, the crew made their way to their Black Widow to prepare for a take-off at 2100 hrs. They would be responsible for covering a large patrol sector that was known to be busy with enemy air traffic, particularly since the start of the offensive.

About 40 minutes into the patrol, 'Marmite' GCI vectored the crew of *"Lady GEN"* towards a bogey flying at 7000 ft (2150 m), which was 3000 ft (900 m) below the normal altitude for a P-61 on patrol. Drop-

P-61A-5 42-5544 *"Lady GEN"* **was crewed by 1Lt Paul A Smith (pilot, seen here in the cockpit) and 2Lt Paul Tierney (radar observer) of the 422nd NFS. The aircraft's scoreboard confirms the crew's haul of five confirmed kills and one probable, one V1 (partially cropped out of this photograph at upper left) and five locomotives. The latter indicate that Smith was also proficient in the air-to-ground role (*John Anderson*)**

ping the nose, Smith eased close enough to get a visual on a Ju 188 twin-engined bomber – a type frequently encountered during the Ardennes offensive. Produced in fewer numbers than the Ju 88, the aircraft could fly at more than 300 mph (499 km/h) and carry a bomb load of up to 6600 lbs (3000 kg). This made it a dangerous threat to Allied troops.

Having received GCI's go-ahead to set up the attack, Tierney took over the pursuit on his radar scope. It was possible that the German aircrew knew that they were in an area patrolled by US nightfighters because the Ju 188 kept making abrupt course changes. These moves probably did not constitute evasive action as such, but represented defensive manoeuvres intended to lessen the chances of being shot down. Its air speed remained at 240 mph (384 km/h) and its altitude was steady.

By the time Smith had locked-on and pulled up into firing range, *"Lady GEN"* had obviously been spotted. The Ju 188 pilot started violent evasive action, which consisted of peeling off, weaving and sudden changes in altitude. It was like trying to track a yo-yo in the dark. Closing to less than 200 ft (60 m) in a hard turn to port, Smith fired a burst of 20 mm cannon with 60-degree deflection. With the element of surprise compromised, an easy straight and level shot was out the question.

The cannon rounds exploded on impact with the Ju 188's canopy area. The intruder straightened out, prompting another quick burst of fire from *"Lady GEN"*, this time with 30-degree deflection. The rounds converged on the Ju 188's starboard wing root, triggering a minor explosion and fire. The aircraft briefly went into a gentle climb, before falling off on its starboard wing. Circling the now descending bomber, Smith and Tierney kept a wary eye on it as its pilot tried forlornly to pull out of the dive. A minute later it hit the ground and exploded.

The P-61 crew said during their debrief that the Ju 188's bomb racks had been empty, indicating that it had dropped its load before its fatal encounter with *"Lady GEN"*. Its initial westerly course, however, tended to contradict the idea that it had completed a bombing mission, for the aircraft would turned immediately to the east once its ordnance was gone.

Photographed during a snow storm at A 78 Florennes in early 1945, this view of *"Lady GEN"* reveals its full mission tally up to that point, as well as the V1 silhouette forward of the row of Swastikas (*Paul Smith*)

Whatever its mission, the enemy aircraft had been shot down at 2210 hrs, just 1 hr 10 min into the P-61's patrol. There was more action to come.

A short while later another bogey was picked up by GCI. This one was much higher, at 17,000 ft (5200 m). In a few minutes Smith had brought *"Lady GEN"* to a position slightly below and to the starboard side of the bogey to enable a positive identification to be made. The contact turned out to be a B-17, however. Immediately after reporting this to ground control, the P-61's crew returned to 10,000 ft (3000 m) to resume their patrol. Smith had just levelled off when 'Marmite' radioed information through about another approaching bogey. Within minutes, Tierney had secured a lock-on at four miles (6.5 km). When the distance had come down to 4000 ft (1200 m), the crew was able to see the intruder, which began taking limited evasive action, probably as a precautionary measure. It was another Ju 188, flying at 9000 ft (2800 m). Again, its bomb racks were also empty.

The enemy pilot immediately took violent evasive action, and Smith fired a burst but it missed completely. The intruder peeled off sharply to starboard and then made a split-S turn to port. The chase was now on. At times hunter and hunted were skimming just 500 ft (150 m) over a snow-covered landscape. Visual contact was lost at least three times during the pursuit, but the P-61's radar remained locked on throughout the pursuit. Another burst found the Ju 188's fuselage and an internal fuel tank was hit, causing the aircraft to erupt in flames. Another burst from 300 ft (900 m) smashed into the right-hand engine, and the wing eventually broke off outboard of the engine nacelle. The bomber spiralled into the ground.

The night's second and, as it transpired, final kill had occurred at 2255 hrs. As Smith and Tierney had shot down a Ju 88 the previous night, they had achieved three confirmed kills within 24 hours.

While the ground situation in the Ardennes remained in doubt for the Allies, the night sky continued to be busy. Herman Ernst and Edward Kopsel had also downed an intruder on the night of 26/27 December. It had been ten days since they had shot down the Ju 87, and with the increase in Luftwaffe activity over the Ardennes, the crew felt another kill was overdue. Flying P-61 *"BORROWED TIME"* on patrol near the Rhine, they had already encountered a Ju 88 that had eventually eluded them after a long chase. This sort of thing often happened at night, and bad winter weather had a lot to do with it.

As the patrol wound down and Ernst prepared to return to A 78, he noticed a lone aircraft flying in an easterly direction at about 2000 ft (600 m) with its navigational lights illuminated. To his amazement, this

Black Widow ace 1Lt Herman Ernst
poses for the camera while seated
at the controls of his P-61 at the
422nd NFS's A 78 Florennes base.
He is wearing a B-8 parachute pack
on his back (*John Anderson*)

aircraft was dropping flares! Using night goggles, Kopsel was able to make a positive identification – it was definitely a Ju 188.

Ernst manoeuvred quickly into position immediately behind the Junkers bomber, but the P-61 was spotted. The enemy pilot took violent evasive action, but it was too late – the range between the two aircraft was less than 500 ft (150 m). The Black Widow's guns spewed 20 mm rounds, and strikes were observed up and down the target's fuselage. The Ju 188's dorsal turret returned fire, and Ernst pulled hard to starboard to both avoid being hit and to prevent overshooting the target. Pulling back astern and slightly below, Ernst fired three more short bursts. Both of the Ju 188's engines were hit, and seconds later they exploded. The intruder fell off to port and went in, being engulfed in a huge fireball when it hit the ground. It was the third confirmed manned kill for *"BORROWED TIME"*, the P-61 also being credited with damaging a Ju 88.

TRIPLE FOR *"DOUBLE TROUBLE"*

Only four P-61 nightfighter pilots became aces during World War 2, but four others came close, each scoring four confirmed kills. If they had been in the right place at the right time they would probably have secured the coveted distinction. Two of the four, 1Lt Robert G Bolinder and 1Lt Robert O Elmore, served with the high-scoring 422nd NFS. Of this small fraternity, only one was able to claim a triple kill in one night.

That memorable mission was flown by 1Lt Bolinder and his radar observer, 1Lt Robert F Graham, during the night of 16/17 December 1944. They were in their Black Widow *"DOUBLE TROUBLE"*. Bolinder explained how it happened;

'That night, our mission was to fly a defensive patrol over an area that was occupied by the American VIII Corps. Halfway through the mission, our GCI radioed that there was an unidentified bogey at a distance of 13 miles (21 km). We immediately closed the gap, and at about three miles (5 km) 1Lt Graham picked it up on his radar scope. We moved up to almost point-blank range, but had still not gotten a positive ID.

'In an effort to move closer I overshot and had to pull a quick 360-degree turn and momentarily lost him. GCI put us back on track and we got to within 100 ft (30 m). That gave us the perfect silhouette of an He 111 flying at about 180 mph (288 km/h). A second later the enemy pilot peeled off sharply to port and went into a complete circle turn, which rolled him right back on his original track. I didn't think we'd been spotted, and that abrupt manoeuvre must have been triggered by a radio transmission from his controller. At that time his course steadied, and I lined him up for a burst with my four 20 mm cannon from a distance of about 400 ft (120 m). It hit him along his port wing root.

'As the intruder's course didn't waiver, I followed up with three more bursts. After the last I had to pull up abruptly to avoid all the debris coming off the He 111. At that moment there was a large explosion as he went into a steep dive towards the ground. I didn't see any parachutes. It was the first kill of that long night.'

Although it was unknown to the Allies at the time, the reason for the activity in the night sky was the launch by the Germans of their last-gasp offensive in the Ardennes. There would be much enemy aerial action for several nights, and plenty of targets for the aircrews of the 422nd. During

1Lt Robert Bolinder and his P-61A-10 42-5565 *"DOUBLE TROUBLE"* are pictured flying above the English countryside days before the D-Day invasion. Crouched behind him is his radar observer, 1Lt Robert Graham. When the war ended Bolinder and Graham had four confirmed kills and a probable to their credit (*Robert Bolinder*)

this period some of the squadron's Black Widows were assigned to protect the US 101st Airborne Division until Gen George Patton could break through the German lines and rescue the troops trapped at Bastogne. But bad weather during the day restricted aerial activity by the USAAF and the Luftwaffe.

1Lt Bolinder continues his account of the action on 16/17 December;

'We carried on patrolling at about 10,000 ft (3000 m) over dense cloud cover, with bright stars above us. We got a call from GCI that an unknown was coming toward us from about 50 miles (80 km) inside enemy territory. It was a fast mover, which indicated a fighter-type aircraft. We picked him up on our airborne intercept radar and closed fast. We were only about 500 ft (150 m) behind him, yet we still couldn't get a positive visual. 1Lt Graham kept telling me the target was at "12 o'clock" and at ten degrees. At last I determined that one of the "stars" moving gently back and forth was not a star, but an Fw 190.

'What I saw was the exhaust from the first single-engined bogey we'd ever encountered. I eased in closer and was able to see the German cross on the side of its fuselage. Easing back, I lined him up and fired a short burst, but didn't observe any hits. For a brief second I thought my gun sight had malfunctioned, so I let go with a long burst that raked the intruder from one end to the other. Most of the rounds went into one of his wing roots. At that point the pilot peeled off sharply to the left and entered a cloud bank. Since we didn't follow him down or see him crash, we were credited with a probable.'

After the encounter with the Fw 190, Bolinder and Graham's regular patrol was over. The aircraft returned to base about 0200 hrs, but due to the squadron's heavy workload its crew were asked to fly another patrol.

By 0330 hrs their fighter had been refuelled and re-armed and was ready to take-off again. Not long after getting airborne, the crew received a report from GCI indicating heavy enemy air activity over the frontlines at below 1500 ft (460 m). Bolinder was vectored right into the thick of the activity and was involved in several chases, as he recalled;

'1Lt Graham's job was very difficult because we were at such a low altitude, which produced an enormous amount of ground clutter on his radar scope. However, he guided me to a good visual. I identified it as a Bf 110, with its prominent twin engines and two vertical stabilisers with large Swastikas painted on them. One burst from my 20 mm guns and the Bf 110 did a quick nose-dive into the ground. Keep in mind that we were very low when we got the visual, and that the intruder's aircrew probably never knew we were there. That was kill number two for that night, along with one probable. But it wasn't over yet. And we didn't have long to think about the Bf 110 because Graham got another lock-on. It put the bogey pretty close to our position, and it only took a few minutes to close and make a confirmed visual.

'We were almost at point-blank range with an He 111 right above the tree-tops. I pulled in behind and just slightly below it. That put us in a dangerous position so close to the ground. It was a no-miss shot with one long burst that ripped into the target. Some of the rounds hit the wing root fuel tank and it was immediately engulfed in a fireball. The stricken aircraft banked sharply downwards. It hit the ground two seconds later, with no sign of any parachutes. There was no way that the crew could have gotten out once I started firing because they were so low.'

Soon afterwards Graham picked up another blip on his scope. *"DOUBLE TROUBLE"* closed in and Bolinder was instructed to make a very tight turn to starboard to get a confirmed visual. Using his peripheral vision, he caught the silhouette of another He 111. By now the two aircraft were so close that they almost collided. Bolinder recalled;

'I thought we'd brushed wings as we were both in the same tight turn in a crossing pattern. Fortunately, as I eased up the He 111 nosed down, and I never saw it again. 1Lt Graham stated that the bogey had gone into a steep dive, probably after he'd spotted us, and more than likely he didn't recover from it because we were so low. We put it down as a kill, but were given a probable.'

Immediately afterwards, *"DOUBLE TROUBLE"* suffered a mechanical failure, obliging Bolinder to return to base. Once on the ground, the crew chief inspected the aircraft closely, but could find no visual evidence of damage caused by the close proximity of the He 111. With the night's patrol completed, the P-61's crew had scored two confirmed kills and two probables. But the story did not end there.

Two months later, 422nd NFS pilot 1Lt James Postlewaite was on leave in England and having dinner with an officer from an engineering company. While exchanging war stories, the engineer mentioned witnessing a German pilot baling out of his fighter in the same area and on the same night as Bolinder had claimed the Fw 190 as a probable. This led to the claim being upgraded to a confirmed kill. The crew of *"DOUBLE TROUBLE"* crew had achieved a unique triple kill that night – their first confirmed kill had come three weeks earlier. Bolinder had come very close to being recognised as the fifth P-61 ace of the war, and

1Lt Eugene D Axtell of the 422nd NFS was the fourth, and last, pilot to become an ace flying the P-61. His five confirmed kills and two probables were claimed between 7 August 1944 and 11 April 1945, and they all came in P-61A-10 42-5568 (*John Anderson*)

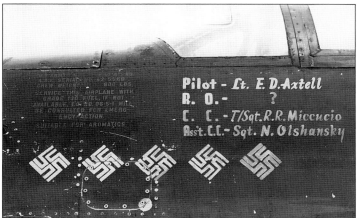

1Lt Eugene D Axtell flew night missions with several different radar observers while achieving his score of five confirmed kills and two probables, hence the question mark below his name in this photograph. The five symbols displayed represent a Ju 88, two Ju 188s and two Ju 52/3ms (*John Anderson*)

he received the Silver Star for his mission on 16/17 December.

The 422nd NFS's outstanding success during the Battle of the Bulge brought further awards and honours for the unit as a whole. The Ninth Air Force presented unit citations to a number of its fighter units during this time frame, but only one was a nightfighter squadron. The 422nd's citation indicated that it had received this decoration for 'outstanding performance of duty in action against the enemy in the Ardennes Salient on the nights of 16/17 December and 27/28 December 1944. On each of these nights the 422nd NFS exerted maximum effort in countering the enemy's attacking forces and, despite extremely adverse weather conditions, succeeded in destroying five enemy aircraft each night. In addition, and above their normal role of intercepting and destroying enemy aircraft, the 422nd attacked marshalling yards, road and rail networks, motor transport and locomotives on intruder missions, thereby effectively continuing their air effort to isolate the battlefield to cover a full 24 hours a day.

'The valiant efforts and unprecedented accomplishments of the 422nd on each of these occasions made a major contribution in denying the enemy his objectives, and constituted an illustrious chapter in the history of the United States Army Air Forces'.

On the same day, Air Medals were awarded to five 422nd pilots, including future five-kill ace 1Lt Eugene Axtell (who had claimed a Ju 88 and a Ju 188 destroyed on 27/28 December, and who would down another Ju 188 on 1 January and then 'make ace' on 11 April with two Ju 52/3ms) and four-kill pilots 1Lts Robert Elmore and Robert Bolinder.

P-61s IN THE PACIFIC

In the Pacific, meanwhile, it was a P-61 Black Widow crew that was to achieve one of the most outstanding nocturnal feats of the war in this theatre. It happened near Mindoro, in the Philippines, on the night of 29/30 December 1944, and involved the 418th NFS. The unit's CO was

Maj Carroll C Smith, whose radar operator was 1Lt Philip B Porter. Together, they formed a uniquely successful nightfighting team. Smith and Porter had been ordered to provide protection for a large convoy anchored off the coast. Over the next few hours they would claim no less than four confirmed kills – two Nakajima J1N 'Irving' nightfighters, one Nakajima A6M2 'Rufe' seaplane fighter and one Nakajima Ki-84 'Frank' fighter. To Maj Smith, the events of that night in 1944 were still etched on his memory almost 50 years later;

'It was a moonless night, with broken clouds at 6000 ft (1800 m) and below. We were on the seaward side of the convoy and under radar control from one of the ships when they vectored us toward an unknown contact. 1Lt Porter guided me in close enough to get a positive identification on a twin-engined Jap aircraft known as an "Irving". I manoeuvred into the best firing position and gave it a burst. To my amazement it immediately burst into flames and nose-dived into the water. By that time we were practically over the anchored ships, so it provided great entertainment for the guys on deck.

'For some reason the Japs were up in force that night because a short time after the first kill, we got another report about a single bogey close by. Again, Porter guided me right in and I fired a quick burst. Another "Irving" went down in flames. The remainder of the patrol was uneventful, and it appeared that we'd had a full night with two kills that were easily confirmed by the people on the ships.'

By now Smith (who had boosted his tally to exactly five kills, two flying the P-38J at night, following his victories during this mission) and his radar operator were exhausted. They assumed that once they landed they could get some sleep, but that would not prove to be the case. As Smith eased the twin-boom nightfighter – as big as a medium bomber, and twice the weight of a loaded P-47 – into its parking area, he was instructed to get back on patrol to fill a gap in the coverage.

The only Black Widow to be flown by an ace (Maj Carroll Smith) in the Pacific theatre was P-61B-15 42-39595 *TIME'S A-WASTIN'*, which was assigned to the 418th NFS (*Carroll Smith*)

TIME'S A-WASTIN' is seen here parked on the airfield on Owi Island, in the Dutch East Indies, ready for another night patrol in September 1944. Maj Smith had yet to claim any of his victories when this photograph was taken (*Carroll Smith*).

The refuelling crew swarmed all over the Black Widow, whose aircrew hardly had time to relieve themselves. Nor was there time to replenish the aircraft's ammunition. Smith and Porter would have to make do with what they had left from the first patrol, but they assumed that by this time of the morning (it was almost dawn) there would be little Japanese aerial activity. They were wrong, as Smith explained;

'We'd been on patrol only a short time when we were vectored toward

another unknown intruder. 1Lt Porter got a contact at about three miles out and had me descend to 500 ft (150 m). We began a chase almost to sea level and then back up to 500 ft. Up and down we went, and for most of the time I had my flaps extended for slow speed manoeuvring.

'About the time that I became convinced that Porter had gone out of his mind, I spotted the "Rufe" about 300 ft (90 m) away. I fired a burst with my 20 mm guns and the bogey exploded and dived straight into the water. My confidence in Porter was once again confirmed. It had been a spectacular kill. I realised that in the future, when he saw something on his radar, I'd best believe him. His range and position information was also very reliable.

'The most frustrating thing was to try to see something of a bogey when Porter kept saying, "He's at '11 o'clock' at 1000 ft – open your eyes, he's there! Try to find an exhaust pattern – get closer! Stay below so you can see his exhaust – hope he doesn't see yours first. Try to get a silhouette against the stars – anything!" I could usually tell by the pitch of Porter's voice on the intercom, as it went up in direct relation to range!

'Finally, a star was momentarily blanked out and I realised why – it was the bogey. Now, to be sure it's the enemy. At this point, my mind wondered back to a similar situation we faced over Morotai when we were vectored on to a bogey. While we were trying to get close enough to identify it, we were fired on by the tail gunner. It had been a B-24, and, thank God, I'd seen those double rudders in time. The aircraft had suffered battle damage and the crew were trying to get back to their base.

'I was roused from my thoughts by our GCI operator, who had another blip on his screen at six miles and 5000 ft (1500 m). By this time it was almost 0700 hrs and becoming light. It was easy to pick up the silhouette. It was definitely a "Frank" – the first one I'd seen. This was the newest Jap fighter, similar to our P-47 Thunderbolt. I was keenly aware that we'd already shot down three aircraft with one load of ammo. Although I thought I had a few rounds left, I couldn't be sure. Since it was getting light, I couldn't run off and hide if I had just made the "Frank" pilot mad!'

Smith kept the P-61 below the Japanese fighter, closing to about 75 ft (23 m) before opening fire. While this was a much closer range than normally required, it was necessary to ensure a fast kill before running out of ammunition.

A close-up view of the artwork that decorated *TIME'S A-WASTIN'*. Note the two victory symbols above the signpost for Los Angeles (*Royce Gordon*)

Four P-61 crews achieved four kills – three in the ETO and one in the Pacific. The latter crew were radar observer 2Lt Raymond Mooney (left) and pilot 1Lt Dale 'Hap' Haberman of the 6th NFS. They were assigned P-61A-1 44-5527, which they duly christened *"MOONHAPPY"* – a name fortuitously derived from a combination of their surnames. Haberman and Mooney downed four 'Betty' bombers with this aircraft (*Dale Haberman*)

What Smith was to witness next was a tribute to the awesome destructive power of the Black Widow's four 20 mm cannon from close range. Within two seconds the 'Frank' had disintegrated. Its pilot had probably not realised what had happened. Small pieces of the Japanese fighter fell towards the water as Smith manoeuvred violently to avoid the debris. The time recorded on his flight log was 0707 hrs. As soon as he had landed, Smith checked the ammunition magazines to discover that 382 rounds had been used, leaving a further 200 unspent! Smith commented;

'When we saw how many rounds of 20 mm we had left, our laughter bordered on the hysterical. I remembered all too well a "Dinah" (Mitsubishi K-46 Army Type 100, command reconnaissance aircraft) I'd shot down over Morotai in a P-38. That took a long time, and I expended 600 rounds. Now, we'd shot down one "Rufe", one "Frank" and two "Irvings", and still had ammo left over. Go figure that out!'

The night's work described so graphically by Maj Smith would have been a rare achievement even by day fighter standards – four kills in one mission. It was probably the most productive mission flown by any Allied nightfighter crew during World War 2, regardless of the theatre of operations.

Compared with day fighter pilots, the achievements of those who flew and fought after dark seem insignificant. But far fewer fighter pilots were trained for nocturnal operations, and as the skies were far less busy at night, their chances of success were considerably lower.

'A DANGEROUS BUSINESS'

The arrival of improved US fighters and better trained pilots in the Pacific in 1942-43 meant that USAAF, US Navy and Marine Corps units flying daytime missions from New Guinea and Guadalcanal were at last able to repel Japanese aerial attacks on Allied bases and shipping in these theatres. This forced the enemy to step up the tempo of night operations, for which the Japanese were well equipped. Having been on a war footing since the mid-1930s, both the Imperial Japanese Navy (IJN) and the Japanese Army Air Force (JAAF) had built up an effective cadre of pilots with night flying expertise.

By mid-1942, enemy bomber pilots were mounting nocturnal attacks on Marine ground troops and Allied naval ships without encountering much resistance. They would fly over vessels anchored around Savo Island and light up the water with flares, while Japanese shore batteries and ship-borne guns hammered the now exposed ships. For US veterans of the early stages of the Guadalcanal campaign, the image of enemy aircraft circling over American ships after dark dropping flares and bombs remains a vivid memory. It was clear that the Japanese bomber pilots were at home in this environment, and their expertise was obvious.

The US Navy's initial efforts to counter these operations involved the use of Consolidated PBY 'Black Cat' flying boats and Grumman TBM

Aircrew from VMF(N)-531 pose for a group photo on Bougainville during 1944. The 20 Lockheed PV-1Ns used by the Marine Corps during this period were the equivalent of the USAAF's P-70 nightfighters, being fitted with AI Mk 4 radar in the nose. Similarly, they were strictly a stop-gap measure intended to intercept the nightly raids mounted by Japanese bombers. The first Naval Aviation nightfighter squadron in the South Pacific, VMF(N)-531 downed 12 enemy aircraft between August 1943 and September 1944 (*USMC*)

The PV-1N Ventura's performance was credible, but as a nightfighter in 1943-44 it was severely lacking in altitude and airspeed capability compared to the IJN's G4M 'Betty' – its principal target. These VMF(N)-531 crewmen represent airborne radar operators (back row) and turret gunners (front row) (*Ed Benintende*)

Cdr William Taylor, a highly experienced nightfighter pilot who had previously served with the RAF (hence the uniform he is wearing in this photograph), was instrumental in establishing at least two US Navy nightfighter squadrons – VF(N)-75 and VF(N)-76 – as part of Project *Afirm*. His expertise was crucial to both squadrons' success in the war (*Tom Cunningham*)

Avenger torpedo-bombers, which targeted Japanese shipping after dark. However, it was clear that the US Navy needed an effective nightfighter force. Yet establishing one was to be an uphill struggle for the officers who were demanding aircraft and pilots able to operate effectively at night. Many senior commanders still believed ship-borne anti-aircraft artillery would provide an effective defence, despite evidence to the contrary.

Some unlikely types were pressed into service as makeshift nightfighters, including the PV-1 Ventura operated by the Marine Corps. VMF(N)-531 began flying combat missions in September 1943 from Banika Island, which enabled them to cover the Russell Island area. But something more effective was already on the way. While the USAAF was opting for a bulky aircraft with a multi-man crew, the US Navy decided that it could manage with something rather smaller.

By late 1943, when the service had received the first of its F4U-2 Corsairs and F6F-3N Hellcats modified as nightfighters, it had a well-established shipboard radar detection and direction system that could be applied to nocturnal combat. Combined with the Sperry AN/APS-6 radar carried in wing-

Nightfighter F4U-2N Corsairs did outstanding work during both day and night missions against the Japanese whilst flown by US Navy and Marine Corps pilots, although none achieved five night kills with the type (*Tailhook Association*)

A nightfighting F4U-2N from VF(N)-101 goes below deck for maintenance after a nocturnal patrol with Task Force 58 in early 1944. The carrier is *Intrepid* (*Tailhook Association*)

mounted pods, this enabled the aircraft to close to within lethal gunnery range. The first of the US Navy's dedicated nightfighter units, F4U-2-equipped VF(N)-75, would not be operational until October 1943, although its first kill was scored before month-end. Sent to airfields in the Solomon Islands, many of VF(N)-75's early Corsairs lacked radar because of a shortage in the number of hand-built sets then available

Ultimately, it would be the Hellcat, supported by the Avengers, that would be the dominate nightfighter type embarked in US Navy carriers in the Pacific for much of the war. The first night kills at sea were credited to Air Wing 6's impromptu 'bat team' aboard USS *Enterprise* (CV-6) on the night of 26 November 1943. Two conventional Hellcats, operating with a radar-equipped TBF-1C Avenger, succeeded in downing two

'Betty' bombers near the Gilbert Islands – the kills were actually claimed by the torpedo-bomber. Tragically, a few minutes later the turret gunner in the Avenger accidentally shot down one of the Hellcats as well, the fighter being flown by legendary ace and Medal of Honor winner Lt Cdr 'Butch' O'Hare, who was the commander of Air Group 6.

The first dedicated fighter unit to deploy to sea was VF(N)-76, which split its complement of radar-equipped F6F-3Ns between Task Force 58 carriers USS *Bunker Hill* (CV-17) and USS *Yorktown* (CV-10) when the vessels departed Pearl Harbor in January 1944. F4U-2N-equipped VF(N)-101 followed suit a short while later when it embarked detachments aboard *Enterprise* and USS *Intrepid* (CV-11).

Although support existed at task force level for night CV operations in early 1944, many air staffs aboard the carriers themselves were reluctant to work deck crews more than 15 hours a day. Nevertheless, VF(N)-76 (split into four four-aircraft detachments that were embarked in four *Essex*-class carriers) made its mark in the Pacific by downing 37 hostile aircraft between February and September 1944. Four of these were claimed by the unit CO, Lt Cdr Pete Aurand.

During this period, VF(N)-76 also played its part in the most memorable aerial action involving US Navy pilots in the Pacific war – the Marianas Turkey Shoot. This action took place on 19-20 June 1944, and a witness to the start of this event was future seven-kill ace Lt(jg) John W Dear of VF(N)-76's Det 2, embarked in USS *Hornet* (CV-12). Although not directly involved in the melee that saw the decimation of the IJN's carrier-based air arm, he had flown a night patrol before the battle started;

'On the night of 18/19 June, *Hornet*'s radar picked up a snooper, and at about 2300 hrs I was catapulted off to intercept it. But as soon as I was airborne the blip disappeared, which put me in a precarious position. None of our carriers was spotted for landing and none was inclined to unload their aeroplanes and re-spot for just one Hellcat. The main Jap fleet had been located, and all of the air groups had more pressing things on their minds!'

Corsair nightfighters of VF(N)-101's Detachment B move into position for a pre-dusk launch from *Intrepid* in late January 1944 – each detachment operated just four aircraft within the air group. The squadron claimed five aerial victories between February and June 1944 (*Tailhook Association*)

This situation presented Dear with two options. He could either remain airborne until the first Combat Air Patrol (CAP) was launched at 0700 hrs, or ditch in the sea. To do this he would have to select one of the screening destroyers on the outer perimeter, attract the attention of its crew, land in the sea ahead of it and hope to be picked up. Destroyer crews liked to rescue downed pilots because they knew they would be well-rewarded with ice cream from the machines installed in the bigger ships! Although a relatively safe one, the ditching option did not appeal to Dear. He therefore decided to do everything he could to keep his Hellcat in the air until he was able to land on his carrier;

'I still had my belly tank, so if I didn't have to chase any snoopers and no emergencies cropped up, I just might be able to put it down on USS *Belleau Wood* (CVL-24), because it was launching the first CAP. If I succeeded, it would be some kind of record because the normal cruising range of an F6F, without taking extreme conservation measures, was about 6+ hours. I had to beat that by at least 1.5 hrs! I selected an altitude of about 8000 ft (2500 m). I leaned the gasoline-air mixture until the engine was wheezing for fuel and retarded rpm to the point that the aircraft would just maintain altitude without an increase in manifold pressure. I then went into a lazy orbit around the outer perimeter of the task group, and prayed! My biggest problem was going to be staying alert.'

As he circled, Dear tuned his radio to an intermediate frequency used by commercial broadcasters, enabling him to pick up an Australian station as well as the Japanese one known as 'Tokyo Rose'. The music kept him awake. After what seemed like an eternity, the first rays of light appeared over the horizon, and with them came radio messages indicating that CVL-24 was preparing to launch its CAP.

Dear's belly tank was now bone dry, and he jettisoned it to reduce drag. When all the aircraft of the CAP had been launched and the deck crews had finished frantically pushing the remaining aircraft forward to make way for his recovery, Dear was at last able to come aboard. All he had to do was to get his Hellcat, with its fuel tanks now almost empty, safely on to the deck, as he recounted;

'I dropped the gear and tailhook as I came abeam of the carrier, increasing rpm a little to maintain altitude. But I was running lean and without flaps. Turning into the crosswind leg, I dropped the flaps, and as I hit the groove the cylinder head temperature started rising fast. I jammed the mixture into full rich, the prop into full low pitch, opened the cowl flaps and took the cut from the Landing Signal Officer (LSO) – all at the same time! The hook engaged and I was safe. But just a few minutes later I learned that aeroplanes from the Jap fleet were approaching the Marianas Islands in large numbers.

'Adm Mitscher (Vice-Admiral Marc A Mitscher, commander of Task Force 58) ordered all aircraft launched. Hundreds left our carrier group in rapid fashion, and each pilot firewalled his throttles. Superchargers were wide open and each aircraft was climbing as fast as it could. As I stood on the deck I couldn't believe my eyes. It was a clear day with low humidity. With all those aeroplanes streaming their heavy vapour trails, it was like a huge loom weaving a blanket that stretched from horizon-to-horizon to become solid man-made overcast. It was the beginning of the Marianas Turkey Shoot.'

Five VF(N)-76 pilots – two of them aces – from Det 2 pose with one of their Hellcats aboard *Hornet*. They are, front row left to right, Lt Russ Reiserer (nine kills), Lt(jg) John Dear (seven kills) and Lt Tom Cunningham (three kills) (*John Dear*)

Hornet Tales was distributed to the carrier's crew, and this cartoon occupied an entire page in the issue of 30 August 1944. The carrier's nightfighter squadron at this stage of the war was the high-scoring VF(N)-76 (*Tom Cunningham*)

Although missing out during the Marianas Turkey Shoot, Dear got his chance on 24 June, when he destroyed three B5N 'Kate' torpedo-bombers during a single sortie. These were not night kills, however, as John Dear recalled;

'On the morning of 24 June, my det commander, Lt Russ Reiserer, and I were sat in the cockpits of radarless F6F-3s borrowed from VF-2, taking our turn to perform the readiness CAP duty, when we were ordered to emergency scramble to intercept a flight of enemy aircraft coming in towards our carrier force. Unlike with the Marianas Turkey Shoot, this time we knew where the Jap aircraft were. This was to be my first encounter with a sizable group of enemy aeroplanes, and my adrenaline started to flow. We were vectored on a course that would see us meet them head-on at an altitude some 3000-4000 ft (900-1200 m) above their formation. It was not long before we spotted them – 18 "Kate" (Nakajima B5N) torpedo-bombers. They were flying in tight formation, with aerial torpedoes strapped to their bellies.

'If I had any real anxiety about the confrontation, it quickly evaporated as the flight leader signalled for us to set up our firing runs. It was a textbook situation, and I'd done it so many times in practice that it seemed as natural and easy as turning a corner in an automobile. We peeled off in turn into a wing-over high-side run, which brought us in vertically toward the bogies. Since I was at the end of our formation, I picked out a target near the end of theirs.

'I'm sure they were aware of us, and that their rear-seat gunners were firing at us, but I was totally oblivious to anything except getting that baby in the gunsight ring. I started firing in medium bursts just outside of the 1000-ft (300-m) range and, amazingly, all the Jap bombers held their formation without wavering. I could see fragments flying off my target as I fired, but not the flames I wanted. So I did what I was told many times in practice not to do – I flattened out my dive until I was directly behind the Jap, still firing.

'Then it happened. The enemy aircraft exploded in a huge ball of flame right in my face. My cockpit cowl was cracked open a couple of inches for ventilation, as it usually was – another mistake – and the flame from that fire stuck its tongue about four inches (10 cm) into the cockpit all around the perimeter of the Plexiglas hood!'

This shock prompted Dear to break off sharply. As he levelled off, he was lined up perfectly with another 'Kate', which was flying straight ahead as if nothing had happened to the other B5N formally in its formation. In a split second, he fired a long burst into the aircraft, which disintegrated in a violent explosion. As Dear glanced around, it seemed to him that the entire sky was filled with huge balls of fire plummeting down towards the sea. The Hellcats had decimated the attacking formation, and many of the US pilots subsequently described the scene as resembling something from a Hollywood movie. The Japanese formation broke up and the torpedo-bombers turned for home, as Dear recalled;

'The retreating remnants were hugging the wave-tops. I pushed over with them and quickly lined up another one. I was in a steep dive and gave him a quick burst. He too exploded, and then I realised I was running out of altitude. I barely managed to pull out as I skimmed the wave-tops. That was close! A couple of minutes later, our flight reformed and headed back to the carrier. We'd suffered no losses and we were all excited. As we got close to home I was thinking about that

The five pilots in the back row of this photograph accounted for numerous day and night kills while flying with VF(N)-76. They are, from left to right, John Dear (ace), Fred Dungan (ace), Russ Reiserer (ace), Tom Cunningham and 'Scoop' Levering (*Russ Reiserer*)

first kill. I was so close, and it dawned on me that if I'd exploded the "Kate's" torpedo I wouldn't have survived the blast. I promised myself that I wouldn't again get that close before firing.

'When I landed and taxied out of the arrestor gear, I looked up at the bridge and there was our air group CO standing next to "Jocko" Clark (Capt J J Clark, *Hornet*'s CO) with his hand cupped over his ear. I held up three fingers and both smiled broadly, giving me the double thumbs up. It was a great feeling. Russ Reiserer got two in that same fight.'

Soon afterwards, Dear discovered that the gun cameras of the F6F he had borrowed from VF-2 for the mission had been loaded with colour film. The camera equipment had been pre-set to operate with the guns instead of through its own separate switch – nightfighters did not carry gun camera film for obvious reasons. Dear commented that some of the film he exposed during his encounter with the Japanese torpedo-bombers in 1944 was later repeatedly shown on television. Particularly spectacular was his flight through the wall of flame from the exploding 'Kate'.

A UNIQUE ACHIEVEMENT

Of all the US nightfighter aces of World War 2, the achievements of Lt(jg) John Dear's detachment commander, Lt Russ Reiserer, are thought to be unique. Not only was his tally of nine kills achieved during both day and night operations, but he was also a member of the exclusive fraternity of fighter pilots credited with five or more kills in a single day.

Reiserer had served with F4F-4 Wildcat-equipped VF-10, embarked in *Enterprise*, in 1942/43, and claimed a solitary victory with the squadron. Following two months with VF-8 in July-August 1943, he became a founder member of VF(N)-76 when it formed. Made CO of the four-aircraft Detachment 2 embarked in *Hornet*, Reiserer would lead his pilots by example, claiming a number of the 27 victories credited to the flight between April and September 1944 – 11 of these were achieved at night. Aside from Reiserer, Lt(jg)s John Dear and Fred Dungan also 'made ace' with Det 2. VF(N)-76's Det 1 on *Bunker Hill* claimed eight kills (four to CO Lt Cdr Aurand) while Det 3 on USS *Lexington* (CV-16) just one.

F6F-5N Hellcat nightfighters of CVG(N)-41 prepare to take-off from *Independence* in late 1944. This air group was credited with 46 day and night aerial victories (*Tailhook Association*)

The F4U-2Ns of VF(N)-101 claimed five kills during the same time. As revealed in this chapter, the bulk of the victories scored by nightfighter pilots in 1944 were scored during conventional daylight missions in radarless aircraft borrowed from fighter units within the air group. VF(N) pilots routinely complained of insufficient time for night flying, and although the successes demonstrated by radar-equipped Hellcats and Corsairs proved the concept worked, carrier captains and the air bosses that ran the flightdecks remained reluctant to respot decks after dark merely to accommodate one or two 'bat teams'.

The reliability of the equipment fitted into the F6F-3Ns and F4U-2Ns also hindered the units' operability, with electronics personnel hard-pressed to meet operational schedules with only four aircraft per det. Carrier captains, therefore, often regarded smart shiphandling and thick flak as the best protection against nocturnal air attack. Nightfighter pilots disagreed, but they needed sufficient aircraft and support to prove their point. Something more substantial than a four-aircraft det per carrier was needed. Fast carriers needed a night air group, and that is what they got.

NIGHT AIR WING

On the night of 17 February, during the carrier strike on Truk Atoll, *Intrepid* was badly damaged when it was hit in the stern by an aerial

A VT(N)-41 TBM-3D departs *Independence* off Ulithi in late 1944. Launching in the late afternoon, the aircraft would then hunt for Japanese shipping after dark (*Tailhook Association*)

torpedo dropped from a Japanese aircraft that had slipped past a patrolling F6F-3N. This attack, and the subsequent achievements of the VF(N) dets in the Pacific, convinced senior officers in the US Navy that full-time night air group was a good idea. By August such an organisation existed in the form of Carrier Night Air Group 41, embarked in USS *Independence* (CVL-22). Consisting of VF(N)-41, with 19 F6F-5s and 14 F6F-5Ns, and VT(N)-41, with nine TBM-1Ds, the air group claimed its first kills on 12 September when future aces Lt William Henry and Ens Jack Berkheimer downed a snooping Ki-46 'Dinah' detected near the task force just after dawn.

The air group's true baptism of fire came on the night of 12/13 October off the coast of Formosa. Plenty of opposition was expected to VT(N)-41's missions against bases on the island, and that is exactly what happened. Torpedo-carrying 'Betty' bombers attempting to make a low-level run on *Independence* were intercepted by several Hellcat night-fighter CAPs that had been launched to protect the task group. Three raiders were shot down, two of which fell to Lt Henry when he intercepted the incoming bogies at very low level. He was awarded the Navy Cross for his actions.

Lt William E Henry was the US Navy's top nightfighter ace of World War 2. He is credited with 9.5 kills – 6.5 of which were scored at night – while operating from *Independence* with VF(N)-41 (*Bill Hess*)

Three nights later the air group launched further Hellcats, which shot down a trio of Kawanishi H8K 'Emily' flying boats at 0230 hrs. One of these fell to Lt Henry, making him Carrier Night Air Group 41's first ace. By the time *Independence* completed its combat tour in January 1945, Henry had increased his tally to 9.5 kills, seven of which were genuine night victories. The US Navy's only other VF(N) night ace, Ens Jack Berkheimer, also served with VF(N)-41, and he claimed 7.5 victories (5.5 at night). Berkheimer failed to return from a night mission over Luzon on 16 December 1944.

Independence's air group had pioneered operations with a large force of nightfighters, and the tactics it formulated were to serve the US Navy well until war's end. Records show that Carrier Night Air Group 41 shot down 46 enemy aircraft, 27 of which fell during the hours of darkness. A string of 'probables' and enemy aircraft listed as 'damaged' was added to the group's achievements.

Carrier Night Air Group 41 was replaced aboard *Independence* by CVG(N)-90, whose VF(N)-90 was equipped with 34 F6F-5E/Ns and VT(N)-90 21 TBM-3Ds. In February 1945 CVL-22 returned to day operations, and CVG(N)-90's units were divided up between *Enterprise* and USS *Saratoga* (CV-3). Supporting operations such as the invasions of Iwo Jima and Okinawa, and strikes on the Japanese Home Islands, VF(N)-90 claimed 36 aircraft shot down (plus five by the TBMs of VT(N)-90 in four months of combat. During the final two months of the war, the protection of the fast carrier force at night was entrusted to CVG(N)-91, embarked in USS *Bon Homme Richard* (CV-31). Its VF(N)-91 claimed nine kills in July-August 1945, including five in 40 minutes on 13 August – the last Allied nightfighter kills of World War 2.

HIDDEN DANGERS

A nocturnal aerial attack was not the only hazard facing US Navy vessels in the Pacific. Lurking beneath the ocean's surface was the deadly

Lt Tom Cunningham poses in the cockpit of his VF(N)-76 Hellcat aboard *Hornet*. Cunningham scored three daytime kills, as well as a probable. He flew more than 30 night missions as member of VF(N)-76 in 1944 (*Tom Cunningham*)

Japanese submarine force, which posed a constant threat to the carriers in particular, and also increased the dangers for fighter pilots operating from them. Returning to their ships after a CAP on a dark night, they would have to grope their way to a safe deck landing with little help from the ship. Turning on the carrier's lights would only invite attack from enemy submarines in the area. But there were times when it was worth the risk.

During the epic Battle of Leyte Gulf in late October 1944, day fighters were launched late in the afternoon on the 25th. By the time they had attacked the enemy force, their pilots faced returning to their carriers in total darkness. On such occasions it was better to risk turning on lights, including powerful searchlights, rather than lose large numbers of aircraft and their pilots through lack of fuel. Yet it was still virtually impossible for returning pilots to identify their own carrier, especially when several were operating in close proximity. This led to confusion, as Lt(jg) John Dear recalled;

'Sometimes they didn't know which carrier to land on so they just got into any landing pattern they could find. The result was that some ships took on far more aeroplanes than they could handle, while others had almost empty decks. For example, one carrier had aircraft parked up to about the tenth wire (there were 12 arrestor wires in all, plus three barriers) and were still taking more. On the other hand, *Hornet,* which was close by, only took on four. Sometimes pilots had to ditch close to the carriers because they'd run out of gas. There were also incidents when our nightfighters were up after dark and met several of the returning day force that were all but lost and guided them safely back to the carrier. Night flying was a dangerous business even when you were trained to do it.'

MISTAKEN IDENTITY

Most nightfighter pilots emphasised the importance of being able to visually identify a suspected bogey. Yet mistakes still happened. Lt Tom Cunningham of VF(N)-76, operating from *Hornet*, recalled a close call during a night mission off Okinawa which could have ended in tragedy;

'One night I was flying a CAP over the fleet when I was vectored towards an unidentified aircraft closing on our ships. I first picked him up on my screen at 25 miles (40 km). The closure rate was very high because he was coming straight at me. In a matter of minutes, the distance had narrowed down to four miles (6.5 km), and then just one mile. At that point, I made a quick 180-degree turn and pulled in on the unidentified aircraft's "six o'clock". When I got right up to it, I was shocked to see it was a B-17 Flying Fortress. The tail gunner never saw me, as he was too busy smoking a cigarette!

'At that point I dropped back and told GCI it was a friendly B-17. To make sure, they asked me to move in close again and read them the tail number. At this position I was at point-blank range, and I read the numbers off to them. Dropping back again, I waited. In a few minutes they radioed me back that it was indeed a friendly, and not to shoot it down! It was disappointing because I'd charged my six guns, and it would have been my first night kill. So I pulled back slightly behind and above the bomber. I increased speed, diving down under it and then zooming up right in front as I pulled a 180. If the pilot or co-pilot were dozing, more than likely the turbulence from my Hellcat woke them up real fast!'

Night flying in any theatre was dangerous, and the weather played a major part in determining the success of a mission. Perhaps the safest part was the flight itself, because take-offs and landings were the most hazardous times. Pilots operating from land bases may have lacked landing aids, but they were fortunate in comparison with US Navy pilots who had to return to carriers often pitching in rough seas.

Nightfighter ace Lt Russ Reiserer of VF(N)-76 is seen here on Okinawa with a captured Japanese A6M-5 Zero. The fighter had been too badly damaged by strafing US Navy fighters to seek a safer base prior to the island falling to the Americans (*Russ Reiserer*)

IWO JIMA

Although the Marine Corps did not make its amphibious assault on Iwo Jima until February 1945, the tiny volcanic island had been under attack by various US Navy air groups on numerous occasions during the previous year. Lt(jg) John Dear participated in many such missions, and has a clear recollection of the tail end of one which could have ended in more damage to his air group than it caused the enemy.

Most of these attacks involved long flights between the target and parent ship to protect the carriers, while its aircraft were flying their mission. Those flown by Dear involved as much flying during the day as after dark. On one occasion, he was flying a pre-dawn CAP from *Hornet* over Iwo Jima, with the strike force following close behind. Dear's job – and also that of nightfighter ace Lt Russell Reiserer – was to help clear the sky over the target area of Japanese fighters. Dear reported;

'The attack on Iwo proved to be very successful, with over 20 enemy aircraft shot down and numerous others caught on the ground. Our small nightfighter detachment returned to the carrier as the weather was getting nastier by the minute. We landed without much difficulty, but by the time the main force returned it was very bad, and this proved to be the most dangerous part of the mission. The aft end of the deck was pitching about 60 ft

Lt Russ Reiserer became an ace while leading VF(N)-76's Det 2 aboard *Hornet* in 1944. He ended the war with nine kills to his credit, the first of which had been scored in January 1943 while serving with day fighter squadron VF-10 (*Russ Reiserer*)

Five Marine Corps nightfighter squadrons were operating from captured islands during the final months of the war in the Pacific. The second-highest scoring of these units was VMF(N)-541, which claimed 23 aerial kills. All bar one of these victories came in the Philippines, where the squadron received an Army Distinguished Unit Citation for its outstanding work. This F6F-3N was one of the Hellcats assigned to the unit at Peleliu in October 1944 (*Glen Bridge*)

The F4U-4N was an advanced version of the Corsair nightfighter. The final variant was the -5N, which saw extensive service during the Korean War in 1950–53 (*Steve Ginter*)

(18 m). It was so violent that the LSOs had to tie themselves down with ropes to keep from being tossed overboard.

'Such conditions were a nightmare for returning pilots, LSOs and deck crews. The inbound aeroplanes had to be brought into the landing groove at precisely the right time. If they reached the point where the "cut" signal was given when the deck was at it lowest point and rising, they would hit it so hard that the landing gear would buckle. On the other hand, if the deck was at its highest point when the cut signal was received, the aeroplanes would float down the deck and miss all the wires. Unless they could gun the engine in time to take a wave-off, they would wind up in the barriers or worse, slamming into the aeroplanes parked forward.'

Lt Reiserer added;

'It was so stormy that the first LSO had to give up because he was experiencing vertigo from the motion of the deck, combined with the lightning flashes on the horizon astern of the ship.'

At this time the *Belleau Wood* was off *Hornet*'s port beam, and some of the returning pilots from VF(N)-76 had seen the difficulties being encountered by the ship's LSO. One pilot on final approach had failed to jettison his external belly tank. He cut power and the aircraft dropped to the deck, which was rising sharply upwards. It slammed into the deck so hard that the fuel tank was smashed and instantly burst into a fiery inferno. The rolling deck spread the burning fuel from one side to the other. For a few minutes it looked as if the carrier itself was doomed. In such rough weather it would have been impossible for another ship to come in close enough to attempt a rescue. But *Hornet*'s deck crew

responded to the crisis and rapidly extinguished the flames. Such hazards were present on every carrier irrespective of whether it was conducting operations during the day or at night.

MARINE CORPS NIGHTFIGHTERS

The first single-seat Marine Corps nightfighter unit to see combat was F4U-2N-equipped VMF(N)-532, which commenced operations from Tarawa in January 1944. As the only Marine Corsairs nightfighter unit in-theatre, the squadron claimed two kills prior to being sent back home to train future nightfighter pilots in June 1944. Like the US Navy, the Marine Corps quickly adopted the F6F-3/5N as its standard nightfighter, and between May 1944 and April 1945, five units were equipped with the Hellcat and sent into action in the Pacific.

The senior, and most successful, Marine nightfighter unit was VMF(N)-533, which claimed 35 kills in 15 months of combat. VMF(N)-541 achieved 23 victories, VMF(N)-542 18 kills and VMF(N)-543 15 victories. VMF(N)-534 operated primarily from Guam and claimed just one success.

By early June 1945, three of the units had converged on Okinawa, or nearby islands, and these squadrons would claim the bulk of their night kills in the coming weeks, as the Japanese targeted Allied vessels preparing for the invasion of the Home Islands. The Marine Corps' two nightfighter aces scored a number of their victories during this period. The first of these individuals to claim five kills was VMF(N)-542 CO, Maj R Bruce Porter. He had previously claimed three daytime kills while flying F4U-1s with VMF-121 in defence of Guadalcanal in 1943.

On the night of 15 June 1945, Porter was flying a routine patrol from his base at Yontan, working a sector designed to protect the fleet from attacks by Japanese bombers and suicide aircraft. His ground controller, operating from the tiny island of Ie Shima, was experienced, and he passed him pinpoint vectors enabling Porter – flying his assigned F6F-5N BuNo 78669, appropriately named *Black Death* – to close on the intruders. It was a particularly dark night, and his patrol sector placed him between enemy territory and US-held Okinawa. He recalled;

'I was sent up to work a pattern at 10,000 ft (3000 m). That put me in a good position to intercept incoming bogies, which usually came in slightly below that. On some of my previous patrols, I'd been able to see flashes of light in the distance, indicating gun battles on the ground. On one occasion, I'd witnessed a fiery explosion in the distance at about my altitude – it was one of our nightfighters scoring a kill over an incoming Jap bomber. After 45 minutes of a monotonous patrolling, GCI came on the radio and said they had a bogey at 15,000 ft (4600 m) and 30 miles (48 km) out. I went to full power to close on it as quickly as I could.

'I was on full instruments, and when the range was less than three miles, I turned on my radar screen – it had been off to preserve my night vision. The vector was perfect, and in a matter of minutes I was on the intruder's tail. Fortunately for me, it was flying straight and level. Seconds later, I picked up a visual of a dull orange glow coming from the aircraft's exhaust stacks. The distance between us was about 300 ft (90 m). At that point I got a positive identification – the contact was a twin-engined JAAF Ki-45 "Nick" nightfighter.'

Marine Corps nightfighter ace Maj R Bruce Porter discusses tactics with fellow VMF(N)-542 pilot 1Lt James Maguire, who is kneeling on the wing (*James McGuire*)

Marine Corps nightfighter pilot 1Lt Albert Dellamano of VMF(N)-533 prepares for another patrol. He downed a 'Betty', a 'Jake' and a 'Sally' in one mission on the night of 24 May 1945 (*Pat Dellamano*)

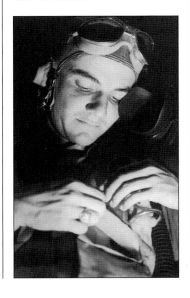

Two of the most experienced Pacific theatre nightfighter pilots pose beside a VMF(N)-533 Hellcat. They are unit CO Lt Col Marion Magruder (left) and his Executive Officer, Maj Homer Hutchinson. Magruder claimed a 'Betty' destroyed on the night of 22 June 1945 (*Ed Le Faivre*)

Two VMF(N)-533 pilots pose with one of their Hellcats on Okinawa. They are 1Lt Ed Le Faivre (left), who scored two kills (a 'Hamp' and a 'Betty', on 18 May 1945), and his wingman, 2Lt Autrey. After the war, Le Faivre stayed in the Marine Corps and flew the F7F-3N Tigercat during the Korean War. He later claimed the 'time-to-climb' record while piloting a Douglas F4D Skyray (*Ed Le Faivre*)

Porter's Hellcat was the only one in the squadron armed with 0.50-cal machine guns and 20 mm cannon. He opened up with both, using his 20 mm sparingly, as the cannon had less ammunition. He aimed for the 'Nick's' right engine and fuselage side in the hope of hitting its internal fuel tanks. Flames duly appeared on the leading edge of the right wing, and seconds later it had spread to the fuselage. Suddenly, the Ki-45 lurched violently to the right as a burst from *Black Death* hammered into its cockpit area. It was over in seconds. Virtually a fireball from nose to tail, the 'Nick' went into a dive. Porter had his first nocturnal victory.

He was still on patrol an hour later when there was a further call from GCI. Another intruder was on the scope at 14,000 ft (4300 m), several miles away. The vector put the interception point dangerously close to the fleet. This would place both aircraft in a free-fire zone for the ships' gunners. Unable to distinguish friend from foe, they would blast away at anything within their area just to be on the safe side. The intruder was heading for Allied ships at an airspeed of 292 mph (467 km/h).

When GCI radioed that the distance was down to 0.75 mile (1.2 km), Porter switched on his radar scope again. Within two minutes, the telltale exhaust flames indicated the target was a twin-engined bomber. This raised the possibility of a tail gunner, so Porter had to approach the bogey with care. Moving closer he identified it as a 'Betty', but one that looked a little different. He explained;

'This one was carrying an external load – a Baka bomb – under the right wing. This was a deadly suicide weapon which was basically a manned bomb. It would be released close to its target, and the pilot would guide it to its quarry. Now, with separation down to 250 ft (80 m), I put the illuminated gunsight pipper between the fuselage and the right engine and slowly squeezed both triggers. A two-second burst caused an instant explosion in the "Betty's" wing tanks.'

Pieces of the doomed bomber trailed back towards Porter's Hellcat, hitting its fuselage and wing leading edges. The Baka blew up, indicating that the flames from the mother ship had reached its volatile propellant tank. The time was precisely 2335 hrs, and Porter had just become an ace. He landed safely at Yontan 25 minutes later, and although it was midnight, the word was out and there was a crowd waiting for Porter when he taxied

to his parking stand. Armourers were then able to determine that he had fired a total of 500 rounds of 0.50-cal ammunition and 200 rounds of 20 mm to achieve the two kills. Until then the unit's average was about 775 0.50-cal rounds per kill. It was evident that the knockdown power of the 20 mm cannon had reduced the number of machine gun rounds fired.

Porter had become an ace, but the distinction of being the Marine Corps' sole true nightfighter ace of the war was to go to Capt Robert Baird. Having completed a combat tour in Corsairs with VMF(N)-532 in 1944, he had returned to the Pacific with VMF(N)-533 in May 1945. The unit had been sent to the Okinawan island of Ie Shima. During the war's final months, this speck of land, just five miles (8 km) long and situated off the northwest coast of Okinawa, was packed with US aircraft. The Japanese became aware of this, and realised that a single bomber would have a good chance of destroying several aircraft. First, though, it would have to run the gauntlet of Allied night patrols mounted by P-61 Black Widows and F6F-5N Hellcats.

Baird claimed his premier kill on the night of 9 June, and followed this up with a further two victories during the early morning hours of 16 June. The first of the latter successes came when, during a routine patrol, GCI told him about a single intruder heading for the island at 23,000 ft (7000 m). Baird was then flying at 10,000 ft (3000 m). He pulled the Hellcat's nose up and increased power to reach an altitude from which a positive identification could be made. Manoeuvring into position, he closed from the intruder's 'six o'clock' to within a half-mile, but the enemy bomber was approaching the firing zone for the anti-aircraft batteries.

Baird was told to back off and orbit, but after pleading his case, he was allowed to continue the pursuit of what he could now clearly see was a 'Betty' beginning its bomb run. Closing quickly to 300 ft (90 m), he squeezed off a short burst, at which point he realised that only three of his six 0.50-cal guns were working. He fired longer bursts, and within seconds the 'Betty' had nosed over in a ball of fire and gone straight down. Baird's mission, however, was far from over.

An hour later, GCI spotted another inbound bogey below Baird's patrol altitude. He responded immediately and got a blip on his radar scope at about 1.5 miles (2.5 km). Manoeuvring into a position to the enemy's side, he made out the silhouette of a Mitsubishi G3M 'Nell' twin-engined bomber. Its air speed was just 180 mph, 288 km/h, and Baird eased back to about 300 ft (90 m) behind it and fired a burst. This time only two of his guns were functioning, but the aim was perfect and his rounds bracketed the starboard engine. It burst into flames and the bomber dived into the sea.

Baird's success resulted in celebrations within the squadron, but he had certainly not finished. Six

Capt Robert Baird was the Marine Corps' only pure nightfighter ace in World War 2, having scored his kills while serving with VMF(N)-533. He remained in the Marine Corps post-war, and flew the F7F-3N Tigercat in the Korean conflict (*Bill Hess*)

Three successful VMF(N)-533 pilots are pictured in front of their tent at Engebi during May 1945. They are, from left to right, 1Lt Al Dellamano (three kills), Capt Bob Baird (six kills) and 1Lt Robert Wellwood (three kills, all of which were 'Betty' bombers downed on the night of 18 May 1945) (*Pat Dellamano*)

The Marines used the nightfighter variant of the Hellcat to establish a remarkable record in the Pacific. They not only operated from forward land bases, but also served aboard carriers towards the end of the war. This F6F-5N from Marine Air Group 24 is shown preparing for a catapult shot from USS *Santee* (CVE-29) just days before Hiroshima and Nagasaki were bombed in August 1945 (*C H Johns*)

days later, during the early hours of 22 June, he was vectored onto two incoming enemy bombers. The first was a Yokosuka P1Y Ginga, code named 'Frances'. Now, with all his guns operating, Baird poured a perfect pattern of fire into the hapless intruder and blew its tail off. The second target was a 'Betty', and he quickly set it on fire. These victories made him the only all-night Marine Corps ace, and he had also become the only nightfighter pilot operating in the Okinawa area to chalk up two double kills.

Early on the morning of 14 July, while flying one of only two new F6F-5N Hellcats equipped with both 0.50-cal machine guns and 20 mm cannon in his squadron, Baird was on the last shift of a night patrol when, at 0441 hrs, he was vectored onto a 'Betty'. This time he came up beneath the enemy bomber and fired a three-second burst of 20 mm fire. He was far enough from the target for his rounds to hit both the bomber's engines. He watched for a few seconds as it flew straight and level, showing no evidence of damage. Then it rolled onto its back and dived straight down. When the 'Betty' passed the 10,000-ft (3000-m) mark the air speed had gone far beyond what the aircraft's structure could tolerate and it broke in half. By scoring his sixth night kill, Capt Robert Baird had guaranteed his place in the history books.

It is perhaps inevitable that the achievements of World War 2 nightfighter pilots should be overshadowed by those who did their flying and fighting by day. They may not have flown arduous bomber escort missions over Germany or decimated the Japanese in massive set-piece engagements like the Marianas Turkey Shoot, but being a nightfighter pilot could be just as hazardous. As ace John Dear pointed out, 'it was a dangerous business. In addition it was often lonely and frequently unrewarding. It also required a high level of expertise – flying a long patrol in the dark and then finding the parent carrier often on a rough night called for a special type of skill.'

By the latter stages of the war, US nightfighter pilots found themselves in control of powerful, heavily-armed machines equipped with the latest electronic technology. This had certainly been the case in the early years of the conflict, but the makeshift P-70s and Venturas were soon to be replaced by the USAAF's powerful P-61 and the radar-equipped Hellcats and Corsairs of the US Navy and Marine Corps.

Their pilots were distinguished by their training and exceptional skill, which made them at least the equals of their Japanese or German counterparts. To achieve the status of ace at night was to join one of the most exclusive fraternities in military aviation history.

APPENDICES

US NIGHTFIGHTER ACES IN RAF/RCAF SERVICE

Nightfighter and Intruder Aces

Name	Service	Unit	Total	Theatre/s
A A Harrington	USAAF	410	7/-/-	UK
C E Edinger	RCAF	410	6/-/1	UK
J F Luma	USAAF	418	5/-/2	UK
C L Johnson	RAF	227	4.5/-/-	MedME
C L Jasper	RCAF	418	4/-/-+3 V1	UK

Nightfighter, Intruder and V1 Aces and other notable pilots

Name	Service	Unit/s	Total	Theatre/s
T G Anderson	RCAF	418	2/-/-	UK
S Cornforth	RAF	23	2/-/1	UK, MedME
P Y Davoud	RCAF	410, 409, 418	1/1/1	UK
E B Edgett	RCAF	272	2/1/-	MedME
G A Holland	RCAF	605	4/-/1	UK
J S Holland	RCAF	46, 227	1.5/-/2	MedME
B F Miller	USAAF	605, FIU, 501	1/-/2 + 9 V1	UK
P T Park	RCAF	89, 108	3/-/-	MedME

Notes
Note that pilots with less than five victories are included because of their inclusion in *Aces High, Stars & Bars* or *Those Other Eagles*, or where there may be doubt as to their actual scores

Theatre Abbreviations
UK - United Kingdom and northwest Europe
MedME - North Africa and Mediterranean

USAAF P-61 BLACK WIDOW ACES

Maj C C Smith (with radar observer 1Lt P B Porter), 418th NFS – 7 kills (includes 2 while flying P-38s) and 2 probables

1Lt H E Ernst (with radar observer 1Lt E H Kopsel) 422nd NFS – 5 kills and 2 damaged (plus 1 V1 destroyed)

1Lt E D Axtell (with radar observers 1Lt B Orzel, 1Lt J U Morris, 1Lt C H Morrison and 1Lt J F Crew), 422nd NFS – 5 kills and 2 probables

1Lt P A Smith (with radar observer 1Lt R E Tierney), 422nd NFS – 5 kills and 1 probable (plus 1 V1 destroyed)

1Lt R F Graham (radar observer, with pilots 1Lt R G Bolinder and Capt R A Anderson), 422nd NFS – 5 kills and 1 probable

Lt R O Elmore (with radar observer 1Lt L F Mapes), 422nd NFS – 4 kills (plus 1 V1 destroyed)

US NAVY NIGHTFIGHTER ACES

Lt R L Reiserer – 1 night kill and 7 day kills with VF(N)-76, and 1 day kill and 2 damaged with VF-10 (in F4F-4)

Lt W E Henry – 6.5 night kills, 3 day kills and 1 probable with VF(N)-41, and one damaged with VS-3 (in SBD-3)

Ens J Orth – 6 night kills with VF-9

Ens J S Berkheimer – 5.5 night kills and 2 day kills with VF(N)-41

Lt(jg) R J Humphrey – 5 night kills and 0.333 day kill with VF-17

Lt(jg) J W Dear Jnr – 4 night kills, 3 day kills and 2 probables with VF(N)-76

Lt(jg) F L Dungan – 4 night kills, 3 day kills and 1 probable with VF(N)-76

Lt K D Smith – 3 night kills with VF(N)-90 and 2 days kills and 1 damaged with VF-82 (in F6F)

US MARINE CORPS NIGHTFIGHTER ACES

Capt R Baird – 6 night kills with VMF(N)-533

Maj R B Porter – 2 night kills with VMF(N)-542 and 3 day kills, 1 probable and 1 damaged with VMF-121 (in F4U-1)

1

**Beaufighter IIF T3145/KP-K of Wg Cdr P Y Davoud,
No 409 Sqn RCAF, Coleby Grange, March 1942**

In early 1942, T3145 was the regular aircraft of the CO, Wg Cdr
Paul Y Davoud, who had claimed the squadron's first victory
the previous November. He flew this aircraft for the first time
on a night flying test on 23 February, accompanied Flg Off
Pynn, and again the following night on a GCI practice. All his
claims, however, were made while flying with Plt Off
Carpenter. Davoud had arrived following the death of
the previous CO while converting to the Merlin-engined
Beaufighter, which could be tricky to handle. Davoud led a
Typhoon Wing later in the war, while T3145 was relegated
to training duties. It crashed in September 1943.

2

**Havoc I BT462/YP-Z of Sgt G R Wright RCAF, No 23 Sqn,
Ford, 21/22 June 1942**

Wright was an American who had joined the RCAF, and
after training was posted to the RAF's No 23 Sqn, flying night
intruder operations. Having arrived in April 1942, he began his
operational career on 7 May and first flew this aircraft (which
had previously served with No 44 Sqn) on the night of 21 June
on an intruder mission to Beauvais. Wright's last sortie in
BT462 was flown on 5 July when he bombed the marshalling
yards at Amiens. He converted to the Mosquito soon afterwards, and it was while flying this type that he claimed to
have destroyed a Do 217. He was, however, lost during
another intruder mission on 7 September, by which time
BT462 had been passed to No 605 Sqn. It was destroyed in
a mid-air collision with another Havoc on 20 July 1942.

3

**Mosquito II DD712/YP-R of Plt Off S J Cornforth,
No 23 Sqn, Bradwell Bay, 15/16 October 1942**

An American from Pittsburgh, Stanley Cornforth had enlisted in
the RAF and joined No 23 Sqn in early 1942. Initially he flew the
Havoc, before converting to the Mosquito – his first mission on
the type, to central France, was flown on 22 August. All-black
DD712 was delivered to the squadron on 8 September and
flown on its first operation, in the hands of the unit's CO, and
ace, Wg Cdr Sammy Hoare, 16 days later. Cornforth flew
DD712 for the first time on 15/16 October when he conducted
an intruder mission to Twente airfield, in Holland. This aircraft
failed to return from its sixth sortie on 29 November.

4

**Beaufighter VIC EL232/J of Flt Lt C L Johnson, No 227 Sqn,
Luqa, Malta, November 1942**

Originally from Oregon, 32-year-old Carl Johnson had a brief
but distinguished career with No 227 Sqn on Malta after joining
the unit in September 1942. On the 25th he claimed his first
success when he shot down a Z.506B flying boat. The
squadron's role was mainly to interdict enemy shipping, and
during one such mission on 14 November while flying this
EL232, he shot down an escorting Bf 109. Johnson quickly
followed this rare kill by downing a Ju 88 minutes later. On 22
November, again flying EL232, Johnson destroyed a pair of

Ju 52/3ms to become an ace. However, the following day,
during an attack on a heavily-armed E-boat, he was shot down
and killed together with his navigator, Sgt R A Webb.

5

**Mosquito II DZ234/YP-Y of Plt Off S J Cornforth,
No 23 Sqn, Luqa, Malta, March 1943**

Stanley Cornforth arrived in Malta to join No 23 Sqn on 16
January 1943, and flew his first mission from the island the
following night when, accompanied by navigator Plt Off
Maurice Davis, he visited attacked airfields. The pair flew
intruder missions regularly, and on the night of 31 January they
encountered a pair of Italian S.82 transports heading for North
Africa. Not only did Cornforth shoot both of them down, he
also chased away their escorting Bf 109. Cornforth and Davis
flew DZ234 for the first time on 8 March on an intruder mission
to western Sicily in poor weather. Repeating that mission two
nights later, they continued to see action through March until
the pair left for an intruder sortie to eastern Sicily in this aircraft
on the evening of 1 April and failed to return.

6

**Beaufighter VIF V8447/N of Plt Off P T Park RCAF,
No 89 Sqn, Castel Benito, Libya, June/July 1943**

After training in Canada, Paul Park was posted to North Africa,
where he joined No 89 Sqn and gained his first two successes
while helping to defend the port of Algiers in late 1942. In early
1943 he claimed his third, and final, success, but continued
to fly defensive patrols from Libya. On 29 June he went on
a dawn patrol in V8447, and that night Park was scrambled for
a further, albeit uneventful, mission. He continued to fly this
aircraft regularly over the next two weeks, the last time being
on 11 July. On 3 August V8447 crashed after a tyre had burst
on landing. The pilot was 17-victory Hurricane ace Wg Cdr
Dennis David, who had just assumed command of the unit.

7

**Mosquito XIII HK465/RA-P of Flt Off R N Geary USAAF,
No 410 Sqn RCAF, Castle Camps, January 1944**

A Californian, Flt Off Dick Geary joined the RCAF nightfighter
unit during the summer of 1943 and started flying combat
operations in October. During the evening of 3 January 1944,
accompanied by Flt Sgt Georges, he took off on a mission from
Castle Camps in this aircraft. Securing a contact in the Bradwell
Bay area, they chased the intruder to the edge of the London
anti-aircraft gun zone before being told to abandon the chase.
Geary flew another patrol in HK465 a few nights later, and
on the 14th was vectored onto a returning Bomber Command
Halifax. On 3 February, he narrowly avoided a head-on collision
with an Fw 190 he had just sighted. Geary's attachment ended
soon afterwards and he returned to USAAF service.

8

**Mosquito VI HJ808/UP-O of TSgt V J Chipman USAAF, No
605 'County of Warwick' Sqn, Bradwell Bay, January 1944**

In the early hours of 3 January 1944, USAAF pilot TSgt V J
Chipman flew one of No 605 Sqn's first sorties of the year
in this aircraft when they undertook an intruder mission to

Melsbroek and the nightfighter base at St Trond. HJ808 was usually flown by ace Flt Lt David Blomely, and displayed its pilot's score. Chipman opened his own account on 19/20 February when he destroyed a twin-engined aircraft at Handorf during an intruder sortie. The following month, and by now a Flight Officer, he damaged a Bf 110 at Laon, north of Paris, and then on the night of 25 April he damaged another twin-engined aircraft on the ground, also at Laon. He was posted back to the USAAF soon afterwards. HJ808 was occasionally flown by another successful USAAF pilot, Flt Off 'Bud' Miller.

9
Mosquito VI HX823/UP-K of Flt Lt G A Holland RCAF, No 605 'County of Warwick' Sqn, Bradwell Bay, March 1944

Although Flt Off 'Bud' Miller regularly flew HX823 in early 1944, the aircraft was also operated by Flt Lt Glen Holland, another successful American pilot serving with the RCAF. On the night of 15/16 March, Holland shot up five trains near Ansbach in this aircraft, but he was killed on the night of 20/21 April. He had made five claims, including four aircraft destroyed, prior to his death. HX823 was lost on an intruder mission to Holland on 23 March.

10
Mosquito FB VI HJ719/TH-U of 1Lt J F Luma USAAF, No 418 Sqn RCAF, Ford, 21 March 1944

Born in Montana, 'Lou' Luma was posted to No 418 Sqn to gain experience of nightfighter operations. He had originally joined the RCAF, and after training transferred to the USAAF. By early spring 1944, usually paired up with Flg Off Colin Finlayson, he had taken his score to three aircraft destroyed. On the evening of 21 March they flew this aircraft in company with another Mosquito on a 'Day Ranger' mission to Luxeuil. The pair created havoc when Luma shot down an ancient W 34 followed by a Ju 52/3m transport to make himself an ace. They then attacked the airfield, and Luma destroyed a Do 217 and an He 111 and damaged four other aircraft. He left the unit soon afterwards and returned to USAAF service, while HJ719 was lost following an engine fire in late June.

11
Tempest V EJ558/SD-R of Flt Off B F Miller USAAF, No 501 'County of Gloucester' Sqn, Bradwell Bay, 24 September 1944

Having flown Mosquito intruders, 'Bud' Miller joined the elite Fighter Interception Unit in the summer of 1944 to operate the Tempest on night interception duties. In July this flight formed the nucleus of No 501 Sqn, which was quickly deployed to counter the threat of night-launched V1 flying bombs. EJ558 was delivered at the end of August, and was regularly flown by Miller, who by that time had already become the USAAF's only 'V1 ace'. He was flying this aircraft on the night of 24 September when he achieved his ninth, and final, V1 victory near Bradwell Bay. EJ558 displayed Miller's score below the cockpit. 'Bud' Miller returned to the US soon afterwards. EJ558 also survived the war, only to be scrapped afterwards.

12
Mosquito XXX MM767/RA-O of 1Lt A A Harrington USAAF, No 410 Sqn RCAF, B 48, Amiens/Glisy and B 51, Lille-Vendeville, October/November 1944

Archie Harrington was another US pilot who had been attached to the RCAF to gain nightfighter experience. On the night of 29 October 1944, he was flying this aircraft, accompanied by Flg Off D G Tongue, when he shot down an Fw 190 near Venlo, in Holland, for his fourth victory. The pair regularly flew MM767/RA-O, and on the evening of 25 November they were vectored onto Ju 88G nightfighter Wk-nr 712295 of 4./NJG 4, which they shot down near Muntz. Almost immediately Tongue gained another contact, and after a chase, Harrington downed a Ju 88G from 5./NJG 4. A third contact resulted in the destruction of yet another Ju 88G a short while later, Harrington's fire having hit its cockpit, engines and wing roots Within an 18-minute period, the American was credited with three aircraft destroyed, taking his final score to seven. Having survived the war, MM767 was duly transferred to the French Air Force.

13
Mosquito XXX MM788/RA-Q of Flt Lt C E Edinger RCAF, No 410 Sqn RCAF, B48 Amiens/Glisy, France, October 1944

An American citizen from Michigan, 'Pop' Edinger enlisted in the RCAF and joined No 410 Sqn in June 1944, making his initial victory claims over Normandy. In September he moved with his unit to France, and flew this aircraft for the first time on the night of 18 October, accompanied by his navigator, Flg Off C C Vaessen. Their three-hour patrol of the Nijmegen area was uneventful, and they continued to fly MM788 occasionally but made no claims. The aircraft was, however, the regular mount of Flt Lt Walter Dinsdale. He was flying it on 27 December when he shot down a Ju 88 over western Germany to claim his third, and final, victory.

14
P-61B-15 Black Widow 42-39595 of Maj C C Smith, 418th NFS, the Philippines, January 1945

TIME'S A-WASTIN' was assigned to the USAAF's highest-scoring nightfighter ace, Maj Carroll C Smith, CO of the 418th NFS, and his radar observer 1Lt Philip B Porter. This crew was credited with five nocturnal kills flying the P-61, while Smith had scored two further successes whilst operating P-38Js in conjunction with ground-based searchlights. This aircraft survived the war and was salvaged on 21 December 1945.

15
F4U-2 Corsair (BuNo unknown) of Maj E H Vaughan, VMF(N)-532, Engebi Island, Eniwetok Atoll, spring 1944

This aircraft was assigned to VMF(N)-532's second CO, Maj Everette H Vaughan, who named it *SHIRLEY JUNE* after his wife. This squadron was the Marine Corps' first single-seat night-fighter unit to see combat, and the only one to achieve aerial kills (two in total) with the F4U-2. It initially went into action over Tarawa, before later being based on Saipan, from where it operated night combat air patrols as far as Guam. The unit returned to MCAS Miramar in late October 1944.

16
P-61A-5 Black Widow 42-5547 of 1Lt H E Ernst, 422nd NFS, Ford, July 1944

The 422nd NFS was able to boast more nightfighter aces than any other USAAF squadron. 1Lt Herman Ernst flew

"BORROWED TIME" with his radar observer 2Lt Edward Kopsel, and scored five kills against enemy aircraft plus one V1 destroyed over the English Channel. This early-build aircraft lacked the upper 0.50-cal machine gun turret supplementing the fuselage-mounted quartet of 20 mm cannon seen on later aircraft. This aircraft was eventually salvaged at Florennes in early December 1944.

17

PV-1N Ventura (BuNo unknown) of VMF(N)-531, Solomon Islands, September 1943

VMF(N)-531 was US naval aviation's first nightfighter squadron to see action, operating PV-1N Venturas hastily equipped with nose-mounted AI MK 4 radar and thrown into action as stop-gap nightfighters. These aircraft were shipped to Espiritu Santo, in the Solomons, aboard the carrier USS *Long Island* (CVE-1) in August 1943. *Eight Ball* was one of the PV-1Ns operated by VMF(N)-531 during the Solomons campaign.

18

F6F-5N Hellcat BuNo 78669 of Maj R B Porter, VMF(N)-542, Yontan, Okinawa, June 1945

Adorned with the name *Black Death* and an artistic rendition of Bruce Porter's favourite tipple (Schenley's whiskey), this cannon-armed Hellcat was regularly flown by the CO of VMF(N)-542 in June 1945. He had inherited it from Maj W C Kellum, the previous commanding officer of the unit. Porter was flying this aircraft when he scored his final two kills on the night of 15 June 1945.

19

P-61A-10 Black Widow 42-5565 of 2Lt R G Bolinder, 422nd NFS, Etain, France, late 1944

By scoring four kills plus a probable in *"DOUBLE TROUBLE"*, pilot 2Lt Robert G Bolinder and radar observer Flt Off Robert F Graham came tantalisingly close to joining the highly-exclusive ranks of American nightfighter aces. They flew with the high-scoring 422nd NFS over western Europe in this P-61A-10, which also lacked the top-mounted 0.50-cal machine gun turret. This aircraft was written off in a landing accident at Liege, in Belgium, on 26 April 1945.

20

P-61B-6 Black Widow 42-39408 of Capt S Solomon, 548th NFS, Ie Shima, Okinawa, spring 1945

Lady in the Dark achieved the distinction of scoring the USAAF's final nightfighter kill of the Pacific war. Assigned to the 548th NFS based on Ie Shima, it was flown by Capt Sol Solomon and his radar observer 1Lt John Scheerer at a time when the unit's primary task was conducting night intruder missions over the Japanese Home Islands and night patrols in the Okinawa area. This aircraft was eventually scrapped at Clark Field, in the Philippines, the late 1940s.

21

F6F-5N Hellcat BuNo 78704 of Capt R Baird, VMF(N)-533, Ie Shima, Okinawa, July 1945

This aircraft was assigned to the Marine Corps' only pure nightfighter ace, Capt Robert Baird, who saw service with two squadrons in the Pacific. Having completed an uneventful tour flying F4U-2Ns with VMF(N)-532 in 1943-44, Baird used his experience to claim six night victories with VMF(N)-533 – the first five came during a 13-day period in mid-June. Baird claimed six of his seven kills in this rare cannon-armed F6F-5N Hellcat .

22

P-70 Havoc 39-753 of the 481st Night Fighter Operational Training Group, Orlando, Florida, late 1943

Built by Douglas as a P-70 from the outset, this aircraft lacked the nose-mounted radar by the time it was issued to the USAAF nightfighter 'school' in 1943 – note the lack of radar antennae in the nose or the flanks of the forward fuselage. It also lacked the 0.50-cal machine guns that supplemented the 20 mm cannon tub in the bomb-bay of later P-70s. *BLACK MAGIC* was featured in a well-publicised photograph flying in formation with a YP-61 (see page 44). P-70s were extensively used in the early stages of the Pacific war, but when the Black Widows finally reached the frontline, they were relegated to stateside training units. 39-753 was sold for scrap in Spokane, Washington, in January 1946.

23

P-70 Havoc 39-768 of 1Lt F Secord, Det 'A' 6th NFS, New Guinea, late September 1943

Among the first P-70 conversions to see action in the Pacific was this example, christened *Dusty*, which featured the nose-mounted radar and a 20 mm gun tub in the bomb-bay. It came from the main production batch of converted A-20G/Js, and was delivered to the 6th NFS to be flown by 1Lt Fred Secord. The unit was initially based in New Guinea following a long over-water flight to Australia. *Dusty* was subsequently damaged on landing at Townsville, in northern Australia, and eventually salvaged in late January 1944.

24

P-61A-10 42-5598 of 1Lt E Thomas, 6th NFS, Saipan, January 1945

The name *"SLEEPY TIME GAL"* was bestowed on several other aircraft operating with USAAF nightfighter squadrons, and this example was assigned to the 6th NFS. It was flown by 1Lt Ernie Thomas and his radar observer 2Lt John Acre, who were credited with two confirmed night kills. They achieved their successes while flying this 42-5598, which was a replacement following the loss of *"SLEEPY TIME GAL I"*. The aircraft featured the dorsal turret mounting four 0.50-cal machine guns, which supplemented the standard armament of four 20 mm cannon in the belly of the crew nacelle. This aircraft was salvaged on 31 August 1945.

25

Beaufighter VIF V8828 of the 417th NFS, Corsica, early 1944

The four USAAF nightfighter squadrons operating in the Mediterranean theatre were the last to receive the P-61 Black Widow, but they had already proved their effectiveness while flying the Beaufighter between 1943 and 1945. *HI DOC*, displaying a *Bugs Bunny* cartoon character on its fuselage, was assigned to the 417th NFS, and initially based in Algeria – it moved to Corsica as the Allies advanced. The squadron was still operating a full complement of Beaufighters when new P-61s began arriving in the MTO in early 1945.

26

P-61A-5 Black Widow 42-5544 of 1Lt P A Smith, 422nd NFS, A 78 Florennes, Belgium, late December 1945

"*Lady GEN*" was an early-production P-61, and lacked the top 0.50-cal machine gun turret. The aircraft was flown by 1Lt Paul A Smith, who claimed four of his five kills with it. His radar observer was 1Lt Robert Tierney, and their successes included shooting down two Ju 88s, one Ju 188, one He 111 and an Me 410. Smith also downed a V1 over the English Channel. This aircraft was written off in a landing accident at Kassel, in Germany, on 5 June 1945.

27

F6F-5N Hellcat BuNo 70147 of Lt W E Henry, VF(N)-41, USS *Independence* (CVL-22), Philippine Sea, September 1944

Lt William Henry was the US Navy's top-scoring nightfighter pilot, and he claimed at least one of his 6.5 night kills in this aircraft. As VF(N)-41's Executive Officer, Henry also flew numerous daytime missions too, enabling him to score three more kills. The squadron's F6F-5Ns were delivered in late September 1944, and they were used for both day and night operations during the Leyte and Luzon campaigns.

28

F6F-5N Hellcat (BuNo unknown) of VMF-511, USS *Block Island* (CVE-106), Celebes Sea, July 1945

VMF-511 served its combat tour aboard *Block Island*, which was the first of the US Navy's aircraft carriers to deploy an all-Marine Corps carrier air group (MCVG-1). The squadron was equipped with newly-delivered F6F-5Ns, and was initially assigned to train for Project *Danny* in the ETO. This was abandoned and the unit was diverted to the Pacific on 20 March 1945. It flew ground attack missions in support of the Australian 7th Division fighting in Borneo, and on the night of 3 July 1Lt Bruce J Reuter scored the unit's only kill of the war when he shot down an Aichi E13A 'Jake' seaplane. The unit later operated in the Okinawa area.

29

P-61A-1 Black Widow 42-5524 of 2Lt M W McCumber, 6th NFS, Saipan, late 1944

The 6th NFS was one of two USAAF Black Widow units whose aircraft displayed elaborate nose art such as the example depicted here. It was also among the first to receive the P-61A-1, deliveries of which started on 1 May 1944. This 'Dash-1' model was one of the few early-build aircraft equipped with the top turret before production of this weapon was diverted to new B-29s coming off Boeing's assembly line. 42-5524 was assigned to 2Lt Myrle W McCumber and his radar observer Flt Off Daniel L Hinz – its gunner was listed as Pte Peter Dutkanicz. This crew is credited with two confirmed aerial kills. This aircraft was salvaged on 31 August 1945.

30

F6F-3N Hellcat BuNo 42158 of Lt R L Reiserer, VF(N)-76 Det 2, USS *Hornet* (CV-12), western Pacific, July 1944

The nightfighter version of the F6F Hellcat was an exceptional aircraft, and the example depicted here was piloted by US Navy ace Lt Russell L Reiserer. He led VF(N)-76's Det 2 to great success during its seven-month spell in the frontline,

the flight of four Hellcats and not many more pilots claiming 27 aerial victories (including 11 at night). During this timeframe its parent unit controlled three dets, and these served on three different aircraft carriers.

31

P-38G Lightning (serial unknown) of the 6th NFS, New Guinea, late 1943

For a brief period during 1943 the 6th NFS operated two P-38Gs equipped with nose-mounted SCR-540 radar, as well as a handful of conventional P-38Js. These aircraft were used as stopgap nightfighters, working in conjunction with ground-based searchlights in New Guinea and on some of the newly-captured Pacific islands. The aircraft were painted in a dull black scheme overall, and were also distinguished from all-silver standard models by the radar antennae protruding from the nose. The P-38 nightfighters also operated with airborne P-70s to help them intercept the high-flying Japanese G4M 'Betty' bombers that flew frequent nocturnal intruder missions over US-held territory.

32

TBM-3D Avenger (BuNo unknown) of VT(N)-90, USS *Enterprise* (CV-6), western Pacific, spring 1945

Although there were no Avenger nightfighter aces, units flying radar-equipped TBM-3Ds did claim a handful of kills after dark. The leading exponent was VT(N)-90's Lt Charles E Henderson, who, during eight engagements in 1945 claimed four kills – he received credit for three confirmed and a probable. Two of his victories came at night. This unit, along with the eight other VT(N)s formed in 1944–45, were the scourge of Japanese shipping in the closing stages of the Pacific war. The TBM-3D was equipped with the then state-of-the-art AN/APS-3 radar installed in a pod on the leading edge of the starboard wing.

33

P-61A-1 Black Widow 44-5527 of 2Lt D Haberman, 6th NFS, Saipan, late 1944

The 6th NFS operated a combination of Black Widows in matt olive drab and black finishes. Replacement aircraft were delivered in an all-black scheme, as seen here on 44-5527 "*MOONHAPPY*". The aircraft was flown by 2Lt Dale 'Hap' Haberman, radar observer 2Lt Raymond Mooney and gunner Pte Pat Farelly, this crew joining an elite group when they were credited with four confirmed kills – just one short of the total needed for elevation to ace status. They did, however, form the highest-scoring team in the 6th NFS, which claimed a total of 16 kills while operating the P-61. This unit was also the longest-serving US nightfighter squadron, and it operated P-61s longer than any other. This aircraft was also salvaged on 31 August 1945.

COLOUR SECTION

1

A number of A-20 Havocs were fitted with radar and cannon and re-designated P-70 nightfighters early in the war. This particular aircraft, boasting Hindu God inspired nose-art, was assigned to Detachment-A of the 6th NFS in New Guinea in the early summer of 1943 (*Fred Secord*)

2

This publicity photograph was taken for the USAAF in 1943 to demonstrate the old and the new in nightfighting. The latter is represented by the new YP-61 Black Widow, while below it is a radarless and well-worn P-70, featuring a weaponless 20 mm cannon tub in the bomb-bay area (*National Archives*)

3

This photograph, taken at night for dramatic effect at Northrop's California facility, shows the P-61 Black Widow's tremendous firepower – four 0.50-cal machine guns in the top turret and four 20 mm cannon in the belly pack (*Northrop*)

4

P-61Bs of the 6th NFS perform a daytime fly-by over Saipan during the early summer of 1945. This was a training flight by replacement aircrews, who were by then entering the war in large numbers. With 16 kills credited to its Black Widows, the 6th was the USAAF's second highest-scoring nightfighter squadron in the Pacific theatre (*Jean Desclos*)

5

I'll Get By was assigned to the 426th NFS in the China-Burma-India theatre, where it was piloted by Capt John Wilfong, who was credited with one kill (*Fred Lefever*)

6

Both USAAF nightfighter squadrons assigned to the ETO were combat-ready soon after D-Day following training in England. 425th NFS P-61A-10 Black Widow 42-5569 *TABITHA* is seen here at a forward base in France, probably Vannes. Note that its invasion stripes have not yet worn off (*USAF*)

7

DANGEROUS DAN was assigned to the 425th NFS, which flew from bases in France after D-Day. Groundcrews are seen here loading 20 mm rounds for the P-61's belly pack (*USAF*)

8

These 419th NFS P-38Gs were flown in a standard dull olive drab over grey scheme whilst briefly operating as nightfighters in the Pacific in 1943. Working in conjunction with searchlight crews, their objective was the interception of high-flying 'Betty' bombers over Bougainville (*Charles Van Bibber*)

9

VMF(N)-541 'Bat Eyes' claimed 23 kills, making it the second highest-scoring Marine Corps nightfighter squadron of them all. Four of its pilots pose here with an F6F-5N on a forward island base in the Philippines in mid-1945 (*Roy Oliver*)

10

VMF(N)-541 personnel display the squadron's scoreboard. Nearly half the enemy aircraft destroyed by the unit were claimed at dawn on 12 December 1944, when 11 Japanese bombers were shot down as they attempted to attack Allied ships in the Philippines (*Roy Oliver*)

11

This F6F-3N was assigned to the advanced nightfighter training programme at MCAS Cherry Point, North Carolina, in the spring of 1944. VMF(N)-541, which was in training when this photograph was taken, was subsequently assigned to the Pacific theatre in September 1944 (*Roy Oliver*)

12

A Marine Corps training command F6F-2N taxies out at the start of a practice mission at MCAS Cherry Point in the spring of 1944. Seven Marine nightfighter units were commissioned at Cherry Point between 1942 and 1944 (*Roy Oliver*)

BIBLIOGRAPHY

Banks, Capt R D, *From Whitecaps to Contrails*. CFB Shearwater, 1981

Bowman, Martin, & Cushing, Tom, *Confounding the Reich*. PSL, 1996

Flintham, Vic, & Thomas, Andrew, *Combat Codes*. Airlife, 2003

Griffin, John, & Kostenuk, Samuel, *RCAF Squadron Histories and Aircraft*. Samuel Stevens, 1977

Halley, James, *Squadrons of the RAF and Commonwealth*, Air Britain. 1988

Jefford, Wg Cdr C G, *RAF Squadrons*. Airlife, 1988 and 2001

McFarland, Stephen L, *Conquering the Night*. USAF Museum, 1997

Milberry, Larry, & Halliday, Hugh, *The RCAF at War 1939-1945*. CANAV, 1990

Nesbit, Roy C, *The Strike Wings*. William Kimber, 1984

Rawlings, John D R, *Fighter Squadrons of the RAF*. Macdonald, 1969

Rawlings, John D R, *Coastal, Support and Special Squadrons of the RAF*. Janes, 1982

Richards, Denis, *RAF Official History 1939-45, Parts 1 and 2*. HMSO, 1954

Rudd, Peter, *The Red Eagles*. Peter Rudd, 1995

Shores, Christopher, *Aces High Vol 2*. Grub Street, 1999

Shores, Christopher, *Those Other Eagles*. Grub Street, 2004

Shores, Christopher, & Williams, Clive, *Aces High Vol 1*. Grub Street, 1994

Shores, Christopher, & Cull, Brian, with Maliza, Nicola, *Malta - the Spitfire Year - 1942*. Grub Street, 1988

Shores, Christopher, Ring, Hans, & Hess, William, *Fighters over Tunisia*. Neville Spearman, 1974

INDEX

aircraft
A6M-5 Zero **83**
A-20 Havoc **1**(44, 94), **56**
A-20G **10**
B-25H **10**
Beaufighter 7–8, 52–54, **53**
  IF **32**
  II **14**
  IIF **7**, 13–14, **13**, **1**(33, 91)
  VIC **31**, **4**(34, 91)
  VIF 14, **14**, **6**(34, 91), **25**(41, 93), **50**, **51**, **54**
Blenheim IF 6–7, **6**
Boulton Paul Defiant I 8, **8**, 13
F4U Corsair
  F4U-2N **15**(37, 92), 74–75, **75**, 76, **76**, 80
  F4U-4N **84**
F6F Hellcat 75–76, **82**, **86**
  F6F-2N **12**(48, 95)
  F6F-3N **11**(48, 95), 74, 76, 80, **84**
  F6F-5N **18**(38, 93), **21**(39, 93), **27**(41, 94), **28**(42, 94), **30**(42, 94), **9**(47, 95), **80**, **88**
I'll Get By **5**(45, 95)
Mosquito
  II 15–16, **16**, **17**, 19, **3**(33, 91), **5**(34, 91), 49
  VI **18**, **22**, **8**(35, 91–92), **9**(35, 92), **10**(36, 92)
  XIII 19–20, **19**, **7**(35, 91), 58
  XVII 27
  XXX **24**, **29**, **12**(36, 92), **13**(37, 92), **52**
P-38 Lightning **31**(43, 94), **8**(47, 95), 56–58
P-61 Black Widow 9, **12**, **7**(46, 95), 55, **55**
  P-61A-1 **29**(42, 94), **33**(43, 94), **72**
  P-61A-5 **16**(38, 92–93), **26**(41, 94), **58**, **60**, 64–65, **64**, **65**
  P 61A-10 **19**(39, 93), **24**(40, 93), **6**(46, 95), 66–69, **67**, **69**
  P-61B **4**(45, 95), **57**
  P-61B-6 **20**(39, 93)
  P-61B-15 **14**(37, 92), **70**, **71**
P-70 Havoc **11**, **15**, **2**(33, 91), **22**(40, 93), **23**(40, 93), **1**(44, 94), **2**(44, 95), 56, **56**
PV-1N Ventura **17**(38, 93), **73**, 74, **74**
TBM-3D Avenger **32**(43, 94), **80**
Tempest V 25–26, **26**, **11**(36, 92)
YP-61 Black Widow **2**(44, 95), **3**(45, 95)

Alford, Capt James E 55–56
Anderson, Flg Off Tom 20–21, 24
Aurand, Lt Cdr Pete 76, 79
Autrey, 2Lt **86**
Axtell, 1Lt Eugene D 69

Baird, Capt Robert **21**(39, 93), 86–88, **87**
Baker, Flt Sgt Frank 30, **30**
Berkheimer, Ens Jack 81
Block Island, USS 94
Blomeley, Flt Lt David 18, 92
Bolinder, 1Lt Robert G **19**(39, 93), 66–69, **67**

Chipman, TSgt V J 18, 21, 22, **8**(35, 91–92)
Cleveland, Howie **22**
Cornforth, Plt Off Stanley J 15–16, **16**, **3**(33, 91), **5**(34, 91), 49, 50
Cunningham, Lt Tom **78**, **79**, 82–83, **82**

David, Wg Cdr Dennis 50, 91

Davoud, Wg Cdr Paul Y 8, 13–15, **13**, 17, **17**, **1**(33, 91)
Day, Flt Sgt Frank **22**
Dear, Lt(jg) John 76–79, **78**, **79**, 82, 83–84, 88
Dellamano, 1Lt Albert **85**, **87**
Dungan, Fred 79, **79**

Edgett, Flg Off Ernest 50–51, 52
Edinger, Flt Lt Charles E 'Pop' 20, 24–25, 26, 27, 30, **13**(37, 92)
Elmore, 1Lt Robert O 60–61, **60**, 62–63, 66, 69
Enterprise, USS 75–76
Ernst, 1Lt Herman E **16**(38, 92–93), 58–60, **59**, **60**, 61–62, 65–66, **66**

Finlayson, Flg Off Colin 21, **21**, 22, **22**, 92

Geary, Flt Off Richard N 16, 19–20, **19**, **7**(35, 91)
Graham, 1Lt Robert 66–68, **67**, 93
Gregor, Flt Off R D S Hank 29–30, **30**

Haberman, 2Lt Dale 'Hap' **33**(43, 94), **72**
Harmer, Cdr R E 'Chick' 11–12
Harrington, 1Lt Archie A 16, 19, **19**, 20, **20**, 24, 25, 26–27, 28–29, **28**, **12**(36, 92)
Henderson, Lt Charles E 94
Henry, Lt William E **27**(41, 94), 81, **81**
Holland, Flt Lt Glen A 18, 22, 23, **9**(35, 92)
Holland, Plt Off J S 'Tex' 51–52, 54
Hornet, USS 76–77, 82, 84–85
Hornet Tales 78
Hutchinson, Maj Homer **86**

Independence, USS **80**, 81
Intrepid, USS **75**, 76, 80

Jasper, Flg Off Murl 19, 22–24, 25
Jeffrey, 2Lt Rayford W 54
Jenner, 1Lt Vernon 57–58
Johnson, Flt Lt Carl L 31, 32–49, **4**(34, 91)

Keeping, Plt Off **28**
Kopsel, 1Lt Edward **59**, 65–66, 93

Le Faivre, 1Lt Ed **86**
Levering, 'Scoop' 79
Leyte Gulf, Battle of (1944) 82
Luma, 1Lt James F 'Lou' 17, 20, 21, **21**, 22, **22**, **10**(35, 92)

MacFadyen, Don 17, 23
McCumber 2Lt Myrle W **29**(42, 94)
Magruder, Lt Col Marion **86**
Maguire, 1Lt James **85**
Mapes, 2Lt Leonard 60–61, **60**, 62–63
Marianas Turkey Shoot (1944) 76–77
Miller, Flt Lt B F 'Bud' 17–18, **18**, 21–22, 25–26, **25**, **11**(36, 92)
Mooney, 2Lt Raymond **72**

nightfighter squadrons and groups
  6th NFS **31**(43, 94), **4**(45, 95), **55**, 56, 93, 94
  414th NFS 53
  415th NFS 53
  416th NFS **52**, 53
  417th NFS **25**(41, 93), 53, 54
  418th NFS 9, 10–11, 56–58, 69–72, 92
  422nd NFS 58–69, 92–93, 94
  425th NFS 58, 59
  548th NFS 93

Air Wing 6 75–76
Carrier Night Air Group 41 80–81, 94
CVG(N)-41 **80**
CVG(N)-90 81
CVG(N)-91 81
Night Fighter Operational Training Group 93
No 23 Sqn 15–16, 49, 50, 91
No 46 Sqn 51–52
No 68 Sqn 27, 28
No 89 Sqn 32, 49–50, 91
No 141 Sqn 29, 30
No 157 Sqn 17
No 227 Sqn 31–49, 52, 91
No 272 Sqn 31, 50–51, 52
No 409 Sqn 13–15, 91
No 410 Sqn 8, 13, 16, 19–20, 24–25, 26–27, 28–29, 30, 91, 92
No 418 Sqn 17, 19, 20–21, 22, 23, 24, 92
No 456 Sqn 27–28
No 501 Sqn 92
No 605 Sqn 17–18, 21–24, 25–26, 91–92
VF(N)-41 80–81, 94
VF(N)-76 76–79, **78**, **79**, 80–81, 82–85, 94
VF(N)-90 81
VF(N)-101 11–12, **75**, 76, **76**, 80
VMF-511 **28**(42, 94)
VMF(N)-531 **17**(38, 93), **73**, 74, **74**
VMF(N)-532 85, 92
VMF(N)-533 85, 86–88, 93
VMF(N)-534 85
VMF(N)-541 'Bat Eyes' **9**(47, 95), **10**(48, 95), 84, 85
VMF(N)-542 85–86, 93
VMF(N)-543 85
VT(N)-41 80–81, **80**
VT(N)-90 **32**(43, 94), 81

O'Hare, Lt Cdr 'Butch' 76

Park, Plt Off Paul T 32, **6**(34, 91), 49–50
Porter, Maj R Bruce 4, **18**(38, 93), 85–86, **85**
Porter, 1Lt Philip B 70–72, 92

radar 7, 55, **55**, 74–75, 80
Reiserer, Lt Russell L **30**(42, 94), 78, **78**, 79, **79**, 83, **83**, 84

Santee, USS 88
Schultz, Flg Off Rayne **19**
Secord, 1Lt Fred **23**(40, 93)
Smith, Maj Carroll C 9, 10–11, **14**(37, 92), 56–57, 58, 70–72
Smith, Lt Paul A **26**(41, 94), 63–65, **64**
Solomon, Capt Sol **20**(39, 93)
Starr, Sqn Leader 'Jackie' **16**

Taylor, Cdr William **74**
Thomas, 1Lt Ernie **24**(40, 93)
Tierney, 2Lt Paul 63–65, 94
Tongue, Flg Dennis 19, 20, 25, 27, 28–29, 92

Vaessen, Flg Off Chuck 24, 26, 27, 30, 92
Vaughan, Maj Everette H **15**(37, 92)

Wellwood, 1Lt Robert **87**
Wilfong, Capt John **5**(45, 95)
Wright, Sgt G R 15, **15**, 16, **2**(33, 91)